ON PURPOSE

HOW TO HELP YOUR GIRL BUILD SELF-CONFIDENCE AND DO ALL THAT SHE'S MEANT FOR IN THE WORLD

DANIELLE FULIGNI MCKAY

MYGIRL
COACHING

Published by MyGirl Coaching LLC

Visit www.girl-onpurpose.com for more information
and to connect with Danielle!

Please note that some names and identifying details have been
changed to protect the privacy of individuals. Occasionally,
dialogue consistent with the character or nature of the person
speaking has been supplemented. All persons within are actual
individuals; there are no composite characters. The material
included in this book is intended for informational purposes only
and in no way is meant to substitute for individualized mental
health therapy by a medical professional. Web addresses or links
contained herein may have changed since publication and may
no longer be valid.

Cover Design by Stephanie Dalzell

First Printing, 2018

Printed in the United States of America

ISBN-13: 978-1986860109
ISBN-10: 1986860108

ACKNOWLEDGEMENTS

Writing this book has been a labor of love—love for my mom, for my two amazing daughters, Margaret and Elizabeth, and for the thousands of girls I've led in confidence-building workshops in and around the Bay Area. In particular, a special group of girls from my eight-week confidence-building series in the Fall of 2017 continually inspired me during the process of writing this book. Here's a shout-out to them—thank you Annabelle, Alyson, Cameron, Nina, Kaitlin, Ella, Sydney, Elizabeth, Allie, Ellie, Olivia, Charlotte, Valentina, and Alyssa. I'd also like to thank my superhero review team—Patricia Fuligni, Caroline Whitehead, Stacey Ward, Adrianne Lee, Jen Bauer, Kristen Hendricks, Renee Haen, Benjamin McKay, Erwin Valencia, Karen (Bon Bon) Bonnar-Faye, Stephanie Masuda and Jocelyn Siegel. Of course, thank you also to my two "Boys on Purpose"—Ben and Gus. And last but not least, thank you Azul Terronez and Ann Maynard for all of your support and guidance and for pulling me through to the very end!

DEDICATION

To my girls: Mom, Margaret, Elizabeth

CONTENTS

PREFACE

From adolescence through my early adult life, I've hated to have the spotlight on me for fear of making a mistake. I never volunteered to speak in front of groups or in class. Presentations? No, thank you. I gave only one presentation during my entire time in college, and on that day I vowed never to give another.

It was a charcoal drawing class I signed up for in the Department of Visual and Environmental Studies while attending Harvard University. I looked forward to meeting every week because it made me feel like I was good at something, whereas I never felt like I measured up in my academic courses. I could see the presentation date looming toward the end of the syllabus, but felt determined to muster the courage to do it well.

It was a studio setting with maybe twenty students, and the lighting was always dim; it was intimate, and my peers were accepting. Our professor, on the other hand, wasn't quite so supportive—at least, not to me. I felt like she didn't like me because I was so quiet. She tended to ignore me, and when she didn't, our interactions were cold, her voice sharp. I didn't pay it much mind; she wasn't my first "tough" professor. Besides, I just loved to come draw and get my meditative fix.

We had been assigned a take-home, 3-foot x 5-foot charcoal landscape as our final project for the semester. I drew mine of the view from my dorm window, which was in a high-rise tower, so my project showed a lot of rooftops and the Boston skyline on the other side of the Charles River. I was really proud of the final product, having never done anything on such a large scale before. It took a long time and I loved how it turned out. To this day, I have it framed in my house.

Then came presentation day, when each student was expected to stand in front of the class to discuss their final project. I steeled myself as much as I could, but as my turn drew near, fear started to tighten its grip. My palms became clammy, goose bumps flecked my arms, and my heart started to beat faster. My breathing became shallow, then stopped momentarily when my professor looked in my direction and said, "Let's hear from Danielle."

My heart raced as I took my place at the front of the room, but I managed to move through my presentation just as I had practiced: what I drew, the materials and techniques I used. Clear. Straightforward. I didn't have a ton to say beyond that. I've never been verbose and have always found it hard to wax on with overly descriptive sentences. It didn't matter; I was almost done. I closed my presentation the way the other students had: "I can now take questions."

The teacher asked me for some clarifications about my work, much as she had with my peers, and I responded briefly. And then she ended my presentation with a simple, shattering question: "Danielle, do you tend toward boredom?"

I stood there stunned. In a small, embarrassed voice, I replied, "No." A deafening silence followed; no one said anything. I wasn't sure if she had humiliated me or not because no one else was reacting.

"You can take your seat," she answered, and moved on to the next student.

As I walked toward my chair, I could feel my emotions getting the better of me. That sting in the inner corners of my eyes, the tightening in my throat, and the quiver in my jaw. I left the classroom quickly after, ran to the bathroom, and cried. I stayed there for a few minutes, standing against the tiled wall in defeat, then splashed some water on my face, took a deep, faltering breath, and walked back to the classroom. I quietly sat back down and tried to pretend nothing had happened.

I remember the long, cold walk back to my dorm cafeteria. Once in the cafeteria, I sat down and ate with a pit in my stomach the entire time. I felt *so* bad about myself that day. I wanted to forget it ever happened, but couldn't. The worst part was I didn't know what to do with how I felt. I never talked to anyone about it, and I had zero tools to process it. I internalized it instead. *Stay quiet. Stay small.* One of my fears to this day is that someone will find me boring. But when I realized that my daughters might one day believe those same things about themselves, I knew I could stay quiet no longer.

INTRODUCTION

What are your hopes and dreams for the young girl in your life? Is self-confidence one of them? If not, it should be. If you want your girl to be and do all that she's uniquely meant for in the world, this book is for you. It will not only give you the tools to help her become comfortable in her own skin, but it will enable you to be the role model she needs you to be.

When I was younger, I used to think self-confidence was something other people had and I didn't. Even worse, I believed you could only be born with it. No one ever explained to me that there were steps I could take to directly build my confidence muscles. Knowing this would have probably changed the course of my entire life. I'm not complaining, mind you, but if I had more self-confidence earlier, I probably would have stood up to that college professor who humiliated me. I might have actually tried out for the *a cappella* group I was dying to be a part of.

And I'm positive I'd have better handled that time in seventh grade when all of my "friends" decided I was no longer cool enough to hang out with them, and I was left all alone. But that's not what happened. It took me until my early forties to start to build my confidence.

I remember the moment in detail because it was such a sudden realization, and I teared up at the thought. I was pregnant with my second daughter, sitting in my office cubicle working away at a job where I didn't feel like I was making a difference. I felt stuck and frustrated. I started daydreaming about my girls and how I would encourage them to be their bold, beautiful selves someday! The only problem was, how on earth could I bring myself to utter such words when I was not doing the same?

I thought to myself, "I am the primary same-sex role model for my girls for how to be a woman on purpose in today's day and age." My next thought was, "I'm not doing a very stand-up job." I knew I needed to lead by example and could see where I was failing to live up to my own ideals. That's when I dedicated myself to making a change.

The first step I took in my confidence journey was volunteering for Girls on the Run (GOTR) at the elementary school down the street, which I found out about from a simple ad online. The reason why this was so important—other than that GOTR is an awesome, confidence-building organization for girls—is because I signed up to be the *head coach*. Not the assistant coach, not the behind-the-scenes person, or whatever other smaller job was available. I purposely decided to do *the* thing that scared me the most: to be the one totally in charge. And to possibly fail big-time because I had no idea what I was doing. I brought all three of my kids with me to the twice-a-week, early-morning practices because I wanted them to see me pushing my boundaries in the same way I hoped they'd extend themselves someday. That spring, I learned more about what it means to be self-confident than the girls in our magical GOTR group probably did. That spring, my inner heroine began to emerge.

As my Girls on the Run experience unfolded, I also did my fair share of researching and studying self-confidence. Then I trained to become a life coach. I applied my findings to myself, getting to know *me* on a new level, respectfully rejecting my inner critic, and continuing to take healthy risks on a regular basis. I also took control of my mindset, my emotions, and my perspective. Not to mention learning to healthily self-soothe and surrounding myself only with people who support my growth. And then, finally, when I felt like I was in a pretty good place, I started teaching others. First women and moms, and then girls. I started leading group confidence-building workshops. I had my daughters again observe me in these leadership positions as I kept stretching outside my comfort zone. And then I folded my girls into the process, where I taught them to practice the same tools I'd been sharing with hundreds before them. Now ages ten and eight, they stand up in front of groups by themselves delivering life-changing content to other girls. Not in my wildest dreams did I imagine this would be the outcome of doing something that scared me.

Perhaps you're a new mom, imagining all of the possibilities for your daughter but in the back of your mind you know it's going to be a jungle out there for her. Or you're already worried as you see your girl's personality playing out in the public sphere, and she's just not grabbing the world by the horns like you know she could. Or maybe you've struggled with self-confidence yourself and are finally realizing that you need to step over your pain and get up and out in order to confidently lead her. **This is your time, and this is your book.**

Girl on Purpose will take you and your girl on a journey both inward and outward. Through practical tools and exercises drawn directly from our workshops, you'll learn what motivates you, what holds you back, what you stand for, what you want, and, ultimately, what you control. **More importantly, you'll find a shared language to use while building self-confidence together with your girl.** It will strengthen your relationship and strengthen you. By the last page, you'll both have what it takes to tie it all up with the messy, beautiful, bright bow called self-confidence. It's the gift you and the special girl in your life deserve.

In the first chapter, I'll get you started with the same experiential process I used to build my own self-confidence so I could help my girls build theirs. I recommend reading the book all the way through once, before delving into it a second time with your girl. From my own journey, I can promise you this won't be the easiest thing you've ever done. However, when you see your girl surprise *herself* with the confidence you build together, all the work will be worth it.

Chapter 1

BECOMING
A GIRL ON PURPOSE

A few years ago, I did an informal survey on Facebook asking people what they want most for their daughters when it comes to self-confidence. I

> "The rising tide lifts all boats."
>
> - John F. Kennedy

received a spectrum of responses from both moms and dads. Some said they wanted their daughter to love and value herself and not look for validation from others. Others replied that it was for her to try new things and take risks without worrying whether her choice will make her unpopular. Still more shared that they hoped she would be optimistic and know she can do anything she sets her mind to, that she'd stand up for what's right and respectfully voice her opinions, and that she would persevere in the face of defeat, set goals, and go after them. My favorite responses? "I want my daughter to break from the pack, do her own thing and know it's good to be different," and, "I want her to value effort over achievement."

Confidence is a topic that all sorts of people (not just moms) *really* care about. I know you do, too. After all, you bought this book for a reason. You know the odds are stacked against you and the important girl in your life when it comes to building self-confidence. In fact, the journal *Science*[i] reported last year that by the age of five, girls believe they are not as smart as their male classmates. Age five! That's scary, but don't get mired in the muck. It's never too early (or too late) to start building self-confidence.

There are many definitions for self-confidence. As you can see, all the people in my survey had varying takes on it. But I can assure you, while confidence encompasses all of those things, it's also *much more simple*. And I'm going to let you in on a few secrets that will not only demystify the concept, but also make it more tangible so that you will feel like it's yours for the taking.

Self-confidence is the ability to be and do all that you want to in the world.
. . . AND be yourself in the process.

I teach this truth to girls all the time in my coaching workshops. At first, they look at me with a stunned expression. But as I explain what it means to simply have the courage to do those things *they* love or want to do and to be true to who *they* are on the inside, the message slowly sinks in.

There's something else I want to point out to you, and that is the crucial role confidence plays in being a girl or woman on purpose. Self-confidence is not about "feeling good," although that does play a role. We have another term for feeling good, called self-esteem. I will delve into self-esteem more in the next chapter. Self-confidence is about *doing* what you want and are meant to do. It's about not being blocked from action by fear, not worrying what people think or trying to be someone else. It is the belief you can do anything you set your mind to, and being true to yourself. In this sense, what it means to be a girl or woman on purpose is never the same for any two people. To have the courage to be Emily is different than the courage to be Caelynn—because Emily and Caelynn are totally unique!

Another tricky thing about self-confidence is that it doesn't always look how you might expect. I tell my students all the time that the confident girl isn't necessarily the popular girl, or the loud girl, or the one getting all the attention. That's what most girls think. Instead, I tell them that this type of girl *may* be confident if that's who she really is and if she's doing what *she* really wants. By the same token, the girl who's quieter, or has fewer friends, or prefers to read, or not be in the spotlight—she can be just as much a girl on purpose as any other girl as long as she's doing what she wants and is being herself in the process.

Confidence is like a muscle. It's a learnable skill, one accessible to anyone! For those of us not born with natural self-assuredness, there is a way to directly build those confidence muscles. Once

> Confidence is "a learnable skill, accessible to anyone."

you know there are things you can do to directly grow your skill, it's simply a matter of choosing to do it, like practice. This book will show you what you can do both for yourself and your girl to build your way up to self-confidence.

Being a confident person is a key component to being a girl or woman on purpose, but it's not the only part worth mentioning. It's also about getting clear on your goals, setting intentions, not second-guessing yourself, and being unapologetic. It includes standing tall from the start and knowing you already have all the natural resourcefulness and creativity you need to tackle any challenge that comes your way. And it's about lighting the path for others and inspiring them to take it, too. After all, a rising tide lifts all boats. Being a girl or woman on purpose is about tying all these things together to live as you want and are called to live. That's what a woman on purpose looks like, and that can be you. And you can show the girl in your life how to live on purpose, as well.

A Coaching Moment

On the heels of seeing the movie Wonder Woman, I was in the pediatrician's office with my ten-year-old daughter Margaret and, I kid you not, the three magazines on the waiting room table were *Boys Life*, *Pregnancy Magazine*, and *Pregnancy & More*. I'm sure this layout wasn't intentional, but Margaret turned to me and said, "I feel like girls are only encouraged to become moms, like that's our main purpose in life. But boys are encouraged to go discover and invent things, to have adventures and be amazing and brilliant." Sadly, what she noticed is still the unspoken message our girls receive on a regular basis. I used the moment as an opportunity to talk about the inaccuracy of the media and that she should pay it no mind. I asked her, "What do *you* think you should do, Margaret?" and she quickly replied, "Make my own decisions about what I should and shouldn't do!" I told her "Yes!" and that "the rest of world just hasn't caught up with all that girls and women are capable of!" And I told her to simply continue being and doing all that *she's* meant for in the world. That is being a Girl on Purpose.

But if our girls don't see any women around them being amazing and brilliant and discovering and inventing things, what are they to expect for themselves? It's your job and mine to show them the way.

Chapter 2

BUILDING SELF-ESTEEM

A client of mine's daughter struggles a little with low self-esteem. I can tell because she always has to be the best at everything and often compares

> Low self-esteem is a roadblock to high self-confidence.

herself to others. She's not totally okay with just "being" and not "doing." She seems to need more stroking, physical affection, and attention in general. She also gets more easily frustrated with herself. To some extent, she was born this way and we may never know the true root of it. There's no foolproof way to give your girl self-esteem. However, there are some things you can do together right now to ensure that your self-esteem level is a building block for self-confidence, instead of a roadblock.

Healthy self-esteem is about feeling like you *deserve* what you want. It's the belief that you have just as much right as the next girl to pursue what you desire and that you are worthy of recognition, respect, and all the good things that come your way. Those with high self-esteem know they are valued as a unique individual. So, in knowing they matter, they believe that they are deserving of what they want.

Conversely, those with low self-esteem don't inherently believe they deserve good things and as a result have a much harder time self-motivating. To some extent, self-esteem can be developed or strengthened just like self-confidence. Low self-esteem is a roadblock to having or developing high self-confidence, and it's always a roadblock to being a girl or woman on purpose.

Coaching Exercise—Identity Pie Plate

One exercise I've found useful comes from Michelle Cove, Executive Director of MediaGirls.org. The MediaGirls organization takes a stand against negative media messaging toward girls and teaches that we all have inherent value. Their Identity Pie Plate exercise is one you can do on your own or with your girl—or have your girl do it alone. I recommend doing the exercise together, so she sees that you recognize your self-worth, too.

To create the identity pie plate, take a paper plate and divide it into eight sections. Next, write or draw eight of your most positive qualities, one per section. These are supposed to be traits that

> "...you don't need to look a certain way, or be popular or great at soccer to matter."

describe who you are—not what you can or want to do. For example, some of the traits my girls came up with are determined, playful, energetic, and fair. We're trying to get at who you are on the inside to reveal your inherent self-worth. In other words, we're trying to show you that you don't need to look a certain way, or be popular, or great at soccer to matter. You are already unique and valuable just the way you are.

The interesting thing about this exercise is that girls and women rarely stop to think about their best qualities.[ii] In contrast, we spend way more time thinking about what's wrong with us. You may think you can't come up with eight qualities, but push yourself. You can and you will. If you are having a hard time, maybe think of some qualities that someone who loves you or knows you well might say about you. If you're doing this with your daughter and you still get stuck, encourage each other and ask each other for examples!

It's totally normal to find this exercise challenging. Once you've finished, though, take turns sharing your identity pie plates by reading them out loud. Maybe even stand up as though you're giving an official presentation. If it feels funny to state aloud your most positive qualities, remember you're not bragging or being boastful. Think of it as just listing facts about yourself. It's also okay if your girl doesn't want to share out loud, because this is mostly about *her* seeing her positive qualities. According to Michelle Cove, "It's essential that girls—and women—understand and can easily define their self-worth, publicly and privately." Self-worth and self-esteem are at the heart of everything we do in life—every decision, what goals we set for ourselves, who we surround ourselves with, and what we truly believe we can achieve.

Now I dare you to display your identity pie plate in a prominent place as your constant reminder that you deserve anything you want in life!

Coaching Exercise—A Clean Slate

If you're a grown woman, the Identity Plate exercise might feel a bit contrived. One reason for this is because you've had years of experiences layered on top of you. You may find yourself thinking that a simple pie plate isn't going to change anything. Some of your past experiences may have stolen from your sense of self-worth. Others may have simply painted you into a box you're not happy with or no longer serves you. The unfortunate result is that you now have some beliefs limiting what's possible in your life. The good news is that having these limiting beliefs doesn't make them true.

Since you're not working with a clean slate, it's a little more complicated to clear a path to healthier self-esteem. What's especially insidious is that some of the ideas limiting you aren't even conscious. That's why I like the following exercise. I suggest doing this one on your own. You can do it with your daughter, too, if she's an adolescent or particularly mature for her age, but it's probably not appropriate for girls younger than nine or ten.

First, you'll want to get a piece of paper and draw a line down the center so that you have two columns. Next, come up with a list of all the different "spheres" in your life and write them in that first column. For example, you might come up with: work, family, school, friends, health, money, etc. Write these categories in the first column but make sure to leave some space beneath each one. Then, under each category, I want you to write as many thoughts as you can think of that are bothering you about yourself or the situation. So, for example, here are some of mine:

Work:
- I'm not qualified to do what I do.
- I'm not doing a good job.
- My income doesn't contribute enough to the family.
- My work doesn't make a difference.

Family:
- My relationship with my husband isn't close enough.
- I should not have moved so far away from my family.
- Sometimes I think I wasn't meant to have three kids. It's hard.

Friends:
- I'm not well-read or light-hearted enough to fit in.
- I'm not good at making friends.
- I wish I had more deep friendships.

Now, here's the game changer. While the negative statements you wrote in the first column may feel true for you, I want you to write something else that feels MORE true in the second column. You may simply write the opposite of what you already wrote, but I challenge you to find a way to express another truth for yourself. If you can't come up with anything, then just move on to the next statement. It may help to see an example, so here is my second list of MORE true statements.

Work:
- My experiences make me qualified to do what I do.
- When I take the time to reflect on my work, I know I'm doing a good job.
- My business contributes to the family in more

ways than monetarily.

- I know in my heart that my work makes a difference.

Family:
- A closer relationship is possible with enough work, it's just not easy.
- Living far from home gave me independence and has enriched my kids' lives.
- At the end of the day, I'd have it no other way.

Friends:
- I'm fitting in with the people I'm meant to be with.
- More deep friendships are possible with more effort.

Now that you've made your second statements, you should feel a little lighter. You've released some of the weight on your plate. You're also clearing a new path to feel more like you, in fact, deserve the things that you want. Now that you've cleared your slate, it's time to fill it with things that enable your self-worth. It's time to start building those self-confidence muscles.

A Coaching Moment

I've done the Identity Pie Plate exercise with my kids on numerous occasions and every time the experience is different. To be sure, they understand why we're doing it. I explain that the qualities they come up with are the things that make them special no matter what. No matter what! Before they get out of bed in the morning, even before they speak, or before they do anything else for that matter, these things remain. In other words, they don't have to "do" anything to prove them.

The first time, we all had difficulty naming qualities and the tendency was to list what we love or are good at (which gets more at values—see Chapter 3 for this). On this particular occasion, my then-seven-year-old daughter Elizabeth wrote down "honest" to describe herself. I found this interesting since she had been going through a rough patch of not telling the truth. So I brought this up. At first, she was upset. But the cool thing that happened was that it opened up a conversation about the difference between the qualities we already have in spades and the qualities we'd like to develop more. We talked about what it means to be honest and that we need to be truthful with others if we want them to treat us the same way. What we finally determined was that honesty is a quality that she already had but wanted to get even better at.

I'm happy to say that with some intention, awareness, and a little bit of effort, she actually has gotten better at being honest. And boy, is she proud of it! The next time we did our Pie Plates she was able to confidently include honesty in her description of herself.

Notes

Chapter 3

FINDING
HER FRAMEWORK

R emember our definition of self-confidence—the ability to do what you want to do *and* be yourself in the process. To know what you really want and to be who you really are, you

To be yourself, know yourself.

need to know yourself on the inside. One of the ways to do this is to identify your core values. What is most important to you?

Values are different from morals or principles, which assume a good and a bad, or a right and a wrong. Values are intrinsic and unique things that are simply important to you. For example, I value alone time, fitness, and hard work, all of which are personal preference and have nothing to do with morality. However, I also value friendships, commitment, and honesty, which do have a certain sense of morality to them. But these things are values and not morals because they are important to *me*. If

"It's important to know and follow *your* core values, not your friend's, partner's or parents'."

friendships were not important to me, then it wouldn't be one of my values, even if I thought it was morally good. Values are just that—something you *value* enough to make space for in your life.

One way to think about the difference between values and morals or principles is that your values are who you are when no one's looking. For example, some people think they should say that spending time with family or giving back are their most highly held values because society considers them good and right. But if you were to take the time to truly evaluate what motivates you, what you make the time to do on a regular basis or how you make decisions, you may find that you more highly value being organized or being well-respected. These are neither good nor bad, right nor wrong. They just are.

Knowing our values is essential to being a girl or woman on purpose. On the one hand, knowing our values allows us to accept and embrace who we are, thereby strengthening our sense of self-esteem. Second, knowing our values provides a framework and compass for choosing paths, making decisions, and moving forward in the world. It's a tool for being self-confident.

We all have a small set of values that make us who we are. The values that you are—*that are you*—live in your core . . . and, as I like to teach in my courses, everyone is solid, strong, and smart at her core. It never wavers, even under pressure. In fact, your closely held values will likely never change, and that makes them a wonderful tool for making important decisions, making new friends, or even getting through hard times.

Again, it is important to remember that Emily's values may not be the same as what matters to her best friend, Caelynn. And that's okay. It's important to know and follow *your* core values, not your friend's, partner's, or parents'. When you act out of your core values, you'll feel a sense of self-confidence. In other words, your confidence stems from you being the most "you." And when you're not in sync with your values, you'll feel that, too. For example, let's say one of your core values is *commitment*. If you were to quit a project, you probably wouldn't feel very good about it, would you? Sticking to your promise feels a lot better. If I am feeling out of whack, I stop and ensure I am doing things that honor my core values, then I'm back to being me again. When our values drive our behavior, we feel both confident and at peace with our actions. But first, you need to discover what those values are.

Coaching Exercise—Mining for Values

There are tons of ways to mine for your values! You and your girl can start by thinking about something you love or love doing. For example, you might love your dog, going to the beach, or painting a picture. I love running, and I always have. Next, think of the reasons *why* you love those things. Your reasons why might include how it makes you feel or what it gives you. Try to dig deeper than just "it makes me happy" or "it's fun." Some deeper examples might be that you love painting because you love being creative, or using your hands, or being alone, or displaying your work for others to see afterward. I love running not just because of the sensation of it, but because it makes me feel strong and healthy, gives me time to myself to reflect, and gets me outside in nature. Running also satisfies my competitive drive and gives me a sense of accomplishment. The reasons why you love something reveal your core values. From this example, I can say some of my values are health, introspection, nature, and hard work.[iii]

When I do this exercise with my girls, I have them divide their paper into three columns, write one thing they love or love doing at the top of each column, and then fill in their "whys." Then they can see what recurring themes pop up across all three. These repeated words are probably core values for them.

You can also mine for values by exploring a favorite memory, a worst moment, or what a favorite day would entail. For example, think of a moment when you felt most alive. What happened? Where were you? Who was there? What did you see, hear, smell, or taste? Another great way to dig out values is to think of something that *really* bothers you. Chances are this something upsets you because a value is not being met. Why does it bug you so much? The opposite of your answer is probably a value.

Or try these ideas (taken from http://www.thecoaching toolscompany.com):

- This week, what did you go out of your way to do and not do?
- What are three must-have things to take with you into a difficult, possibly dangerous, situation?
- What is your favorite animal and why?
- What is your favorite activity and why?
- Who do you admire and what about them do you admire?

For each of the above, keep asking yourself, "What's special about that?" until you get to a value.

Lastly, you could simply select from a values list. Make sure to articulate what you mean by each of the words you choose, and then rank them from one to five to reveal which sit at the top. The more you're in touch with this core group of values, the more you can draw from them.

Note: Some words may seem redundant, but there are small, important distinctions. Spend as little or as much time on this exercise as you like. I pulled this list from the book *Co-Active Coaching, 2nd Edition* (2007) by Whitworth, Kimsey-House and Sandahl. Also, feel free to add any others you want.

Humor	Participation
Directness	Performance
Partnership	Collaboration
Productivity	Community
Service	Personal power
Contribution	Freedom to choose
Excellence	Connectedness
No obligations	Acceptance
Focus	Acknowledgment
Romance	Friendship
Recognition	Spirituality
Harmony	Empowerment
Accomplishment	Integrity
Orderliness	Creativity
Moving forward	Independence
Honesty	Nurturing
Success	Beauty
Accuracy	Authenticity
Adventure	Risk
Lack of Pretense	Peace
Zest	Elegance
Tradition	Vitality
To be known/seen	Trust
Growth	Health
Aesthetics	Personal Impact

Great job! Now that you've taken some time to distill what matters to you most, do you feel like you know yourself a little bit better? Thinking back on your life, do some of the choices you made or things that you did make more sense? Now keep a list of your top values in your back pocket as a reminder for when you need it most!

Coaching Exercise—Intelligent Questions

The way we talk to young girls matters and can help her discover some of her core values. Rather than commenting on her hair, nails, or outfit, ask her what she's reading, her favorite sports, or what great adventures she's had recently. Generating intelligent conversations with girls not only shows that you respect her brain over her appearance, but it's great modeling. You might start appreciating yourself in new ways, too! If you can change the way you converse with your girl, you can help her understand her values in a more organic way than filling out a list. These kinds of talks will help her identify and own her strengths.

Create opportunities for this by asking her questions about her activities. You can ask her direct questions, such as what she likes and dislikes. Depending on her age and maturity, you could ask her what she perceives as her strengths and weaknesses. Or inquire about her opinions on a subject or her beliefs. She is never too young to start having these kinds of conversations. The best part is getting to watch her face light up when she realizes you consider her thoughts valuable.

One easy way our family asks this kind of question is to keep a stack of Table Topic Cards (http://www.table topics.com) in our kitchen, and I will ask my girls, at random, things like, "What is your dream job and why?" "What is your proudest accomplishment?" "If we were to remodel the house, what would you do first?" "What do you enjoy or miss most about being single?" They have responses to these questions! And it may sound silly, but even if they don't have an answer at the moment, they keep thinking and tend to come back with a response later.

Establishing an understanding of values is essential to this environment of open conversation. If your girl is young, be intentional and transparent about what your family values are so she knows what kinds of things you're talking about—things like cooperation and kindness. You could even write them on a chalkboard in the family room so that they're always visible. With less forthcoming adolescents, you can help by being more covert and asking them to relate to their favorite celebrities or characters in books and discuss what qualities they share or admire most. Asking questions like these will help tease out hidden values.

It also helps to model curiosity by asking her questions purely for the sake of *her* self-discovery. The best questions are not the ones with a yes-or-no answer. Instead, these kinds of questions are expansive, and usually start with the words "what" or "how." So instead of saying, "Did you like the game?" ask, "What did you like about that game?" or, "How would you play differently next time?" Questions fueled by curiosity evoke personal exploration and develop her curiosity and resourcefulness, which is learning that lasts. By doing these kinds of things, you'll further help her define who she is and what she values.

Coaching Exercise—Aligning Lifestyles to Values

Knowing your values is useful, but only if you use that knowledge to act on them! Aligning your actions with your values takes attention to your choices, and one way to keep that vision in mind is goal setting. You can establish a series of value-based goals to work toward—short, medium, and long—so that you can have a constant aim to align with those values. You can do this alone, with your girl, or with your entire family!

The best way to establish these goals is to be transparent and make it fun. If *adventure* is one of your core values, do something adventurous together every weekend and then build up to some big adventure by the end of the year. Or maybe *making a difference* is a core family value. Try regularly participating in volunteer events and then work up to organizing one of your own. Taking a values-based approach realizes an alternative form of success, and shifts the focus to the process instead of trying to score on continually moving goal posts.

Learning your values and incorporating them into everyday life grows your self-confidence because you're living, practicing, and reinforcing who you are at your core. You can then rely on this framework to simplify your decision-making processes, get through difficult times, and live your everyday life. For example, there are nights when I'm exhausted and don't want to go to book club. However, when I remember that one of my highest-ranking core values is *connection*, I go to the meeting despite my fatigue and am always glad I did.

Core values can help your girl make decisions, too. On separate occasions this year, both of my daughters sat themselves out of soccer practice—one with a hurt ankle and the other with a chest cold—because even though they held high values of having fun (what kid doesn't?) and being there for their teams, they also knew how important their health was to them. Your girl can also use values to prioritize her extra-curricular activities when there's not enough time to do it all—and we all know there's not enough time!

A Coaching Moment

While our deepest core values remain fairly consistent throughout our life, their order of priority may shift depending on the circumstances. There was a time last year when Margaret, who was nine, was invited to do something special with her best friend on the same day that she had a soccer game. Margaret loves soccer, but she also adores this friend. It was a hard decision and I was leaving it up to her. The soccer game was not a championship match, but she still had to evaluate her priorities in order to decide what to do. She said she knew if she went to the soccer game she would be honoring her values of being active, being a contributor to her team, and her sense of commitment. She also knew that she would have a great time because she always does when she plays soccer. And while friendship is also a value of hers, she rationalized that playing soccer that day would also be spending time with friends. Soccer is ultimately what she decided to do.

Interestingly, when we recently talked about this moment in retrospect, Margaret said that if she had to do it all over again she thinks she would have made a different decision. Specifically what she realized is that deepening a special friendship is now a higher value of hers than the other values she listed earlier. What she further learned about herself once we started talking is that it's become more important for her to have "me" time and to be able to totally be herself, which is how she feels around this special friend.

Either way, using values to navigate an important decision is a foolproof way to feel like you're being true to yourself and making the right choice in that moment. It eliminates any second-guessing and builds confidence in your decision-making.

Notes

Chapter 4

DEVELOP HELPFUL
SELF-TALK

One day my youngest daughter, Elizabeth, said to me, "If I can change my mind, I can change my reality." She had no idea how wise those words were. Our thoughts become our reality, and it's no secret in the world of psychology that a positive (but realistic) inner monologue is vital to our well-being. We tend to think that things outside of ourselves are what hold us back. But when it comes to low self-confidence, **the main culprit is our own thoughts.**

> "Whether you think you can or you think you can't, you are right."
>
> - Henry Ford

While the last chapter was all about your unchanging inner core, this chapter is about what's changing all the time—your thoughts. This may well be the most important chapter in this book, so take heed!

What is self-talk? Mainly, it's how we make sense of the world. It starts naturally and audibly as toddlers walk around narrating the mechanics of the world. "I am going to put this block over here. I set it on top of the chair." As we get older, our talk moves into our head because we no longer desire to advertise our thoughts to the rest of the world.

When I explain self-talk in my workshops, I find it helpful to first discuss thoughts in general. We are always having thoughts—which is to say, we have thought after thought after thought! Even as you're reading this book, you may also be thinking, "What am I going to do for dinner later?" Or, "I love this exercise!" Or, "I have no idea what she's talking about." I also like to point out that we control how long our thoughts linger. We can fixate on one thought as long as we want, or move onto another one. It's totally up to us. And finally, I always make it clear that thoughts in our head are *just thoughts*. They have nothing to do with our core.

These thoughts we say to ourselves may be positive, negative, or simply neutral. Often, they encompass evaluative statements, including feelings and opinions about ourselves and others. Watch out! These evaluative thoughts are the ones that can really impact you. Some of what we say can take on a negative, bullying tone, even when things might be going our way. For instance, thinking, "If I were really smart I would

> "Gremlin thoughts only gain power over you when you *choose* to believe them."

have gotten an A+," or, "She's so much better than me." There are many names for it (like *saboteur, monkey-mind*, or *inner-bully*), but I like the term "gremlins." I've found this particular word useful because having girls visualize a furry little creature in their head helps them grasp the concept of an inner critic. Some girls even name their gremlins, like Teddy or Claire, as research shows that the act of naming feelings and emotions has a direct effect on how the brain processes emotions and stressors[iv]. To be honest, everyone has gremlins, that critical eye inside that scrutinizes everything. The most valuable tool I offer women and girls is identifying *their* gremlin thoughts.

Sometimes, gremlin thoughts come from the outside. For example, my friend's twelve-year-old daughter Natalia had a soccer teammate who berated her every time she tried to make a play. "You're a loser!" "Why did you do that?!" or, "You're terrible!" she would yell. This girl was a real-life bully that embodied Natalia's gremlin. Natalia tolerated her verbal abuse for years and thus started to internalize some of it as her own self-talk. Most of the time, these thoughts go by unnoticed, even when there is an outside source. Some gremlin thoughts may be outright rude, like, "I'm not smart enough, pretty enough, or good enough." Some, however, may not even sound negative at all, like, "I'm too tired, too busy, or not ready." The most common gremlin thoughts of all are so subtle we don't even realize we're thinking them: "I can't" and "I'm too scared."

Girls are particularly vulnerable to gremlin thoughts. It is interesting to note that differences in brain structure may make girls more self-critical than boys. Joann Deak's research in *Girls Will Be Girls* (2003) shows that the limbic system, which houses the amygdala (otherwise known as the emotional center of the brain), appears to be more sensitive and active in females. In other words, females' thoughts are more frequently and intensely integrated with the emotional system than most males' thoughts are. Deak writes that "in everyday activity, a girl views the moment with both the rational *and* emotional parts of her brain, so that seemingly unemotional situations contain an emotional component for her." And, for a young girl, rising estrogen levels mean the prefrontal cortex is developing, which makes them more empathetic and discerning of the world, but also more self-judging. Lastly, girls can have perfectionist tendencies, which make them critical of themselves when things go wrong.

That's exactly when gremlin thoughts show up! Most often, it's when we're on the verge of taking a risk, getting outside our comfort zone, entering familiar territory where we've had a previous bad experience, or as a result of a failed plan. These gremlins' purpose is simply to distract us and stop us from doing what we want to do. But here's the kicker—your gremlin thoughts only gain power over you when you choose to believe them[v]. In other words, negative self-talk makes us less confident. We control our thoughts; don't let it become the other way around.

In fact, **negative thoughts can shut down your brain**. My husband is always telling our kids that getting upset shuts down your brain. It's his way of helping them not get frustrated when they make a mistake, lose something, or can't figure out their homework. It turns out he's right. In a 2015 article, I read about a brain imaging study where subjects were asked to identify the sex of a person's face when the image was embedded in the center of a photo of a house (it was designed to be an easy question to answer). Those with induced negative or neutral emotional states used only the "face-processing" part of their brain, whereas those with induced positive emotional states used both the "face-processing" and "place-processing" parts of their brain. Isn't this amazing? In other words, the study showed that a negative or neutral state of mind actually narrows your brain's focus, whereas a positive state of mind literally allows you to see the bigger picture!

Negative and neutral states are like having blinders on. Positive states take away the blinders and expand our view and awareness, enlarge our minds, and make the world bigger. If your girl knows that her brain can function more comprehensively when in a positive state of mind, she can use this to her benefit. Imagine the implications when taking a test, playing in a soccer game, or just having a really important conversation. I call this "priming the pump" and tell the girls in our workshops they can do it by simply thinking of something they're proud of or that makes them happy right beforehand. The more you choose to talk to yourself positively and create a positive state of mind for yourself, the more resilient and resourceful you will become. **Practicing positive self-talk can permanently change who you are and how you function.** The key is not getting hooked by your gremlin thoughts and entrenched in negative self-talk.

Some describe self-confidence as a natural state for everyone. We are separate from our thoughts, both negative and positive, and we can see thoughts as simply passing through our minds like clouds. Your mind is your brain in action. Your thoughts and feelings make up your story, but they are not actually you. Whether or not to engage with and get hooked on your thoughts, especially the negative ones, is something we can actively choose.

Coaching Exercise—Unhook the Gremlin

One way to unhook from your gremlin thoughts is to expect and accept them. Evolutionarily, the inner-critic is here to stay and not going anywhere. We are wired to look for the negative and what "could" go wrong. Thousands of years ago, it was a matter of survival for our ancestors, searching for food and escaping predators. Today, most of us no longer face such life-or-death situations, but our bodies and brains still act this way. In fact, experts say that emotional patterns are ingrained in our gray matter as neurochemical memories, which can be triggered again and again under similar circumstances.

Considering this, try to view your gremlin as an undesirable family member or a familiar face that just keeps showing up. Then proceed to simply greet it and politely ignore it! Put some distance in between you and those thoughts, and it will help you stay free from the gremlin's grasp. Accept that gremlin thoughts happen, and then move past them in pursuit of growth and change. As you become aware of negative thoughts, ask yourself, how is this useful to me or helping me? Am I getting closer to my goals? Questions like these can help you put things in perspective and clearly see the choice you're making and its impact.

Some other fun (and funny) ways to create mental distance from negative thoughts and see them for what they are can be found in Russ Harris' *The Confidence Gap* (2011), including:

- To notice your thoughts instead of judging them as good or bad
- View another person saying the thought
- Sing it or say it in a silly voice
- Imagine it typed across a computer screen
- Imagine hearing it as a radio broadcast
- Visualize it as graffiti on a building
- Visualize it as a caption on a greeting card
- Visualize it as movie credits on the big screen

Remember that practice makes perfect. This will be hard at first, but it will get easier! There's a popular saying in neuroscience that what fires together wires together. What this means is that the more often you think a certain way, the more inclined you will be to continue to think that way. In other words, the more traveled a route becomes in your brain, the more it becomes a default pathway. The converse is true, too. As you practice stepping over your gremlin, you will get better at it, and your gremlin route will become a back road you hardly ever travel.

Coaching Exercise—The Inner-Coach

You can teach yourself and your girl how to develop a great inner-coach voice by audibly modeling it or talking to your girl as if you are her coach. Simply trading negative self-talk for positive, or reframing the situation, can be powerful. I was reminded of this one day when I complained to my husband, "I'm a bad parent," and he replied, "You're a good parent having a bad day."

Below are some other marks of a great inner-coach:

- **Always use your first name, or the pronoun "you."** Research from the University of Michigan[vi] shows that calling ourselves by name or by the pronoun "you" rather than "I" creates distance, allowing us to better hear our own advice as if it's coming from a trusted friend. For example, saying to yourself, "Jen, you can do it," (if your name is Jen, of course) is more believable to our psyche than saying "I can do it." In addition, studies show that when using the second or third person in self-talk we're better able to gain control of impulses, focus our attention, and bounce back from failure.

- **Speak with compassion and kindness.** Speak to yourself like you would have another speak to you. An idea your girl might relate to is to teach her to be her own best friend. Ask her how she would talk to her real best friend. Does she support her? Compliment her? Comfort her? What kinds of things would she say? Give specific examples, such as what would she say to her friend who's learning to ride a bike for the first time? What kinds of things wouldn't she say to her best friend? Now, turn those helpful statements inward. Also, when your daughter's inner critic speaks, defend her and say, "Don't talk about my daughter that way!" It will surely teach her to notice the kinds of things she says about herself.

- **Be specific with direction and praise.** Sweeping instructions like, "Try harder," are not as helpful as, "Kick the ball with the inside of your foot." Likewise, general compliments such as "nice work" not only say little, they are unconvincing and not motivating. Instead, say something like, "Great work kicking the ball with the inside of your foot."

- **Maintain a positive, resilient attitude.** Do not get mad at yourself for making mistakes. Instead, use missteps as learning opportunities.

- **Body posture also matters.** Amy Cuddy's book *Presence* (2015) is built around the idea that how you hold your body is a source of personal power. She writes about both sighted and blind runners crossing the finish line with arms up in a V because it is hardwired to put our bodies into open and expansive positions when we feel powerful. As it turns out, the opposite might be true, too. When we make ourselves more open and expansive *first*, we, in turn, feel more confident. A reason for this might be because "bigger" positions raise confidence hormones like oxytocin and decrease stress hormones like cortisol. In our workshops, we teach this idea to girls as a tool for feeling more self-confident in the moment. When feeling doubtful, you can simply sit or stand up straight, shoulders back, and reap the hormonal benefits!

Coaching Exercise—Stubborn Gremlins

Sometimes it's just plain hard to identify your gremlin thoughts, and just plain hard to not get hooked by them. Awareness is the first step, and writing down every thought you have in five minutes is a simple exercise to become more aware of the constant messages we are telling ourselves all day long. Asking these questions might help:

1. What metaphor can you think of for having thoughts running through your mind all day long?
2. Do you notice all of your thoughts?
3. How do you feel different when you tell yourself something positive versus something negative?
4. When do you notice you have negative thoughts the most?

For girls (and women!) with extra stubborn, recurring gremlin thoughts, write them on a piece of paper and either tear it up, bury it, stomp on it, or, one of my favorites, put it in the middle of a busy road and watch cars crush it (but be careful)!

An additional cool visual is to draw a picture of what your gremlin looks like on a piece of "magic" rice paper (I get mine at https://www.sciencebobstore.com), and place it in a bowl of water. Poke at it with a pen, just like you might poke at your actual gremlin thoughts to decide if they're true or not, and watch it disintegrate before your very eyes! The lesson here is that gremlin thoughts "don't hold any water" once we start challenging them.

A Coaching Moment

When my daughter Margaret was six years old, she already had her share of demons. One weekend, she came to me and said, "Mommy, I'm a bad girl." Normally, I would have sympathized with her and said something along the lines of "No you're not!" which would get us nowhere as she'd refute every piece of evidence I'd point toward to the contrary. But this time, I decided not to engage in the debate. Instead, I said, "Honey, what does it do for you to tell yourself you're a bad girl? What's the point? I mean, what does it get you?" To which she quite honestly replied, "It gets me hugs and kisses." (God, I love my Maggie!) So then I said, "Well, why don't you just ask for hugs and kisses if you want them?" Again, honest reply, "Because it's so embarrassing!" Then I stated "Oh, I disagree. I think it shows great strength and courage to ask for what you want and need." There was a pause. A thoughtful look. And then, "Mommy, can I have some hugs and kisses?"

Notes

Chapter 5

EMPOWER HER
CHOICES

C hoosing our thoughts and ignoring our gremlins is important, but this chapter will expand the discussion to the concept of choice and perspective. **We always have a choice.** Let me repeat that. We *always* have a choice. Each one of us has the

> "I discovered I always have choices and sometimes it's only a choice of attitude."
>
> - Judith M. Knowlton

ability to choose how we look at things, situations, people, life, and ourselves. Even in seemingly unchangeable circumstances, we can take back some control and confidence by choosing our attitude and reaction. In other words, not only do we control our thoughts, we control our perspectives, too. The realization that we always get a choice is both empowering and confidence-building. **And it's a critical tool for you and your girl.**

Often when we feel trapped or stuck in life, it's because of the perspective we're standing in. Perspective is a powerful filter that causes us to see only certain things. More than that, we do it to ourselves! Your perspective is not someone else's fault. The great news is that if we have the power to get ourselves stuck, it means we also have the power to get unstuck.

Five years ago, I faced the sudden reality of moving my family and myself cross-country. I didn't want to go, but I also felt like I had no choice. My husband got a new job—a great opportunity, in fact—and my rational mind knew that the adventure would be exciting for all of us. However, I LOVED my life: my job, my friends, my neighbors, where we lived, and all I focused on was how sad I felt to leave them all behind. I could only see what I was losing and not what I would be gaining. I was stuck. But then I decided to try something different and think about the move from a positive, optimistic angle. The first thought that popped into my mind was, "Who knows, maybe one of my new neighbors will end up being the best friend of my entire life." And BAM! This startling idea began to totally shift my perspective. I wondered what other possibilities might await. I asked myself, what if I approached things from the idea that "life could be *even better*!" And this was the difference I needed because it enabled me to finally embrace the journey as MY choice, too.

Some of you might say, "What about when you don't have a real choice?" I'm pretty sure my daughter doesn't think she has a say in a lot of things, and I'd agree. For example, she may think she has no choice about brushing her teeth or going to school—and she's right. A better way to alert her to her power is to admit, "Yes, you're right," and then say, "But you DO have a choice in how you show up to school. Will you attend willingly with an open mind and positive attitude? Or will you complain and blame your parents for making you go?" Again, it's a choice of perspective.

Our perspective also affects how we react to things that happen to us. You may have a girl who's emotionally reactive or stubbornly set in her ways. Both are choices of being. It may seem overly simplistic to suggest she choose a different way of being, but next time you or she over-reacts or is unwilling to try something new, ask, "How is that working for you?" or, "What does it cost you to react that way?" The thing is, she can keep her habits and old ways, but a change in perspective will change her reactions and thus her mode of being.

Try challenging her to see a different path. Ask, "But why not try a different choice *once*? Just for kicks, for fun? As an experiment?" Why not, if the old perspective is not working anyway, right? Help her see her perspective as a tool, something she can control to affect the outcome of her day. If she dreads going to school, challenge her to envision how the day could play out differently with a new perspective. Dare her to start the day with a brighter attitude.

A simple way to illustrate the power of perspective is to tell the old "goldfish in the fish bowl" story. In this tale, the owner places a glass wall down the center of the bowl so that the goldfish only has half a bowl to swim in. After some time, when the owner removes the wall, the fish continues to swim in only half a bowl because it never thinks to check whether the wall is still there. The story is analogous to what happens in our own lives when we don't question our limiting thoughts or hidden assumptions. Try telling this tale (or even drawing a picture of it) to your girl and see how she reacts!

By coaching your girl to see choice and perspective as tools, she can then use them to feel more in control of life and more trusting of herself. THIS is confidence building. She'll learn how to give herself choices, how to no longer be victim to other people, circumstances, or her thoughts. It puts *her* squarely in the driver's seat.

Making these kinds of choices builds self-confidence. Decision-making in and of itself is confidence building because we feel more in control. Raise your girl's awareness about this so she can empower those choices. Point out the choices she has all day long, as well as the consequences. For example, show her she can choose what

> Using choice and perspective as tools "puts her squarely in the driver's seat."

to do with her free time, or whether or not to study. More important than pointing out obvious choices, however, is helping her to see the implicit choices she has in being able to choose her attitude and who she's becoming.

Coaching Exercise—Daily Choosing

Try the following exercise with your girl. Recite out loud the litany of things you have scheduled to do or have already done. List every single minute detail. When we do this exercise in our workshops, the girls only have to say three items to keep it simple. Something like, "I got out of bed," "I ate breakfast," and "I brushed my teeth." For you, it might be "I drove my kids to school," "I have to go to the bank," and, "I will make dinner for my family tonight." You can say actions you've already taken or that are in the future. It doesn't matter.

Next, put on a pair of sunglasses to signify that you're changing perspective then repeat the exercise by prefacing each task with the words "I choose" or "I chose." So for example, with the above activities you would say "I chose to drive my kids to school," "I choose to go to the bank," and "I choose to make dinner for my family tonight."

Chances are, the first time through your list you felt some heaviness, maybe stress or a sense of obligation. You may have even said the words "I need to" or "I have to" before some items. Now after the second time prefacing each statement with "I choose" or "I chose," what felt different? Hopefully, you noticed more lightheartedness. Maybe you felt more positive. More intentional. And more like there are other options and possibilities and that the choices of your day are more up to you than you think.

Coaching Exercise—The Gratitude Attitude

You can take the Daily Choosing exercise one step further by implementing gratitude. Gratitude, or a feeling of appreciation or thanks, is another choice available to us. Actively seeking gratitude is a simple choice we can make which provides a positive perspective or outlook from which we draw self-confidence. In our workshops, we have the girls do the listing exercise a third time but prefacing each statement with "I get to." For you it might be, "I get to drive my kids to school," "I get to go to the bank," "I get to make dinner for my family." Feels pretty fantastic to have those choices in the first place, doesn't it? When my daughters want to change their mood, I tell them to ask themselves what ten things they feel grateful for, and, in no time, they go from feeling glum to being on top of the world.

After trying all three lists, talk about how each perspective felt differently and why. Ask your girl how she can use her "I choose to" and "I get to" glasses in different situations.

Coaching Exercise—The 30,000-Foot View

Another tool you can use with your girl is the 30,000-foot view. Sometimes when we're stuck in the weeds of a situation, taking a step back to see the big picture can help us know what's truly important and what we really want to do.

For example, a friend's daughter wasn't happy in chorus because she thought the teacher was disorganized and didn't have the attention of the students. She wanted to enjoy it, but felt frustrated and wanted to quit. She also wanted her parents to do the quitting for her. Luckily, her parents said she needed to do it herself. The daughter had to step back and think about what was important to her and her reasons why she was quitting before talking to the teacher. The process allowed her to take ownership of her decision and she ended up giving her instructor some helpful feedback! This kind of analysis from afar can help the big picture become clear, and allow new perspectives to shed light on the situation.

A Coaching Moment

Like many kids her age, back in kindergarten, Margaret was resisting doing her homework, which she'd characterized as *boring with a capital B*. So I thought I might try some balance coaching to help her see another side. Balance coaching is when someone stuck in a particular perspective attempts to view an issue through a different lens in hopes of some clarity and forward movement. I use this technique with my clients, so I thought, "Heck, why not try it with my kid?" I asked Maggie to tell me about something she enjoys, and she picked a recent play date with a friend named Julie. I said, "Now tell me what you liked about the play date. What qualities would you use to describe it?" She came up with "fun," "not boring," "having company," and "someone to hang out with when mommy's too busy." I could tell this last one was especially important to her. Then I said, "Well, Maggie, how about trying to see your homework as a friend—fun, not boring, having company, and someone to hang out with?" And that's just about all it took because she was off naming her pencil Writey and her homework Bob. The following week she completed her homework two days early!

Another Coaching Moment

Several years ago, my then-four-year-old was complaining about how much she hates going to preschool. She did this every day she attended, which incidentally was only twice a week! So I said to her, "Okay, Elizabeth, tell me everything you hate about school and don't leave anything out!" I could hardly believe it when she responded enthusiastically! She went on and on about *everything* not to her liking. And by the end of it, she had spoken about six different topics in general. Then I said, "Okay, Elizabeth, you just told me about six things you don't like about school. Now I want you to tell me *at least* six things you *do* like about school." And guess what? She told me eight. She went on to have a fantastic day.

Once you choose to stand firmly in a particular perspective, it becomes a self-fulfilling prophecy. It's like the Law of Attraction and the universe conspiring; the world is full of energetic vibration. Ask your girl if she has ever been in a bad mood that just keeps getting worse and worse throughout the day, then remind her that the opposite can be true, too. If you stay at a positive and powerful frequency, your "vibe," so to speak, the rest of your day will follow that energy level. The power of choice can impact your world, what you pay attention to, those around you, your relationships, who you are, and who you become.

Notes

Chapter 6

GIVE HER THE GIFT OF EMOTIONAL CONFIDENCE

So now that we know we can control our thoughts and perspectives, it's time to learn to control our emotions. Emotions are some of our most powerful experiences, and it's vital that we learn to trust and not second-guess ourselves. In addition, girls

> Some days "I just give myself permission to suck...I find this hugely liberating."
>
> - John Green

need to know that *they* control their emotions, not the other way around. I did not truly learn this truth until I was in my early forties!

I start our workshops on emotional confidence by telling girls several mind-blowing facts:

1. **Emotions are simply waves of energy running through your body.** In other words, they're energy in motion. And they're just information—internal signals on how to behave or respond to thoughts or situations. They help us figure something out.

2. **All emotions are okay.** They are neither good nor bad, right nor wrong. Some people think they should never feel mad or sad, but that's not true. They're your emotions, and you have them for a reason.

3. **Emotions are the physical footprints in your body of thoughts in your head.** Every emotion is *preceded* by a thought. In other words,

> "Your thoughts are fuel for your emotions."

your thoughts are *fuel* for your emotions. Next time you're feeling mad or sad, try tracing backward in your mind and notice the thought(s) you had right beforehand.

4. **The energy wave of an emotion lasts about ninety seconds.**[vii] That's right, ninety seconds! If something you're feeling lasts longer than ninety seconds, it's because you keep having the kind of thoughts that generated the emotion in the first place. So, a simple way to change the way you're feeling is to change what you are thinking.

Explaining to your girl that she can control her feelings because she can control her thoughts—she is not simply at the mercy of her emotions—can be very empowering for her. It can also help her take more responsibility for her mood and reactions. For example, we pointed this out to a girl who once showed up to one of our workshops in a bad mood and it helped her switch outlooks and participate more. This is not to say that we should constantly distract ourselves from feelings we don't want to have by just changing our thoughts. Plus, simply changing our thoughts may not *always* work. Understanding *what* we're feeling is also powerful.

An essential aspect of learning to control your mood is **expanding your emotional range**. By that, I mean understanding the intricacies of the emotions you feel so you are better able to identify them. There are several simple things you can do right off the bat to help your girl expand her emotional range:

1. Enrich her emotional quotient by using more emotion words yourself. For example, instead of saying, "Isn't it great we're all spending the day together," try, "It makes me so happy that we're all together today."

2. Ask your daughter how she is feeling. If she replies with simple answers like, "Fine," prod her to further define what she's feeling. Say, "Fine— good? Fine—bored? Fine—mad?"

3. If your daughter is upset, ask open-ended questions and let her fill in the blanks. Examples are, "What's going on inside?" "How did the game go?" etc.

You can also expand your girl's emotional range by explaining to her the difference between "inside" and "outside" feelings, as described by Rachel Simmons in *The Curse of the Good Girl* (2010) and at The Girls Leadership Institute (http://www.girlsleadership.org). All of the main emotions—happy, sad, mad, scared, and disgust—these are all "outside" feelings because you can see when someone is feeling them. They show on the outside. But did you know they are all felt second to inside feelings? What I mean is that before you feel mad, sad, disgust, etc., you first felt something else more tender and complicated on the inside. Your secondary, outside feeling is just hiding or protecting it.

For example, think of the character Riley from the movie *Inside Out*. When she was talking to her old best friend on her laptop, and the girl told Riley that she made a new friend, Riley got mad and slammed her laptop shut. If you watch closely, you'll see that before getting angry Riley first felt something else more tender—she felt hurt. She was probably thinking that *they* might no longer be best friends, but she tried to hide the hurt she felt inside by being mad on the outside. It may have done Riley some good to stop and notice how her thoughts were creating her emotions.

Other inside feelings we might try to hide are embarrassment, nervousness, feeling disrespected, or jealousy. Knowing the difference between inside and outside feelings is one way to understand your emotions better. You can practice peeling back the outer layer of what you think you're feeling and ask yourself, "What am I feeling closer to my heart?" Doing this will also help you understand and empathize with other people better, especially when you're in an argument with someone. In these situations, try to imagine the emotions the other person might have on the inside, but not show outwardly. Being able to identify and talk about these inside feelings can get to the heart of a matter and diffuse a situation.

I mentioned earlier the importance of your girl knowing that *all* feelings are healthy and that there are no right or wrong ones. A lot of times girls think "negative" feelings are inherently bad, wrong, or inappropriate; and they deny themselves of having them because of that! By challenging her conception of "negative" emotions, like being mad or sad, you allow your girl to be free from guilt whenever those things happen. After all, they happen to everyone, and she has a choice how to handle it. She needs to know that **she has a right to feel *whatever* she feels**—and that she's feeling it for a reason, particularly when it comes to "negative" emotions. Perhaps try to help her see them as an essential body part that is hurting, and if it's ignored or never tended to, the injury will just fester and get worse.

While she has a right to whatever she feels, your girl also needs to know that **she doesn't have a right to *act* or *react* however she wants**. Negative feelings are only "bad" if followed by destructive action, like hurting someone else or hurting ourselves. I always give the example of the time I got angry and yelled at my coworker. Feeling anger was okay; the yelling was not. Same with feeling sad. The sadness is okay. But what's not okay is staying in bed all day and not eating. How your girl reacts is another area where you can teach her to simply feel and observe the emotion without judging it. Instead of lashing out in the heat of the moment, teach her to sit with herself for a minute first and allow a better perspective to wash over.

Finally, one of the best ways to build your girl's emotional confidence is to validate her distress with empathy by saying, "I understand," or, "That must really hurt." This is a hard one for a lot of moms, especially when our girl overreacts and her emotional experience does not reflect reality. But you need to strike a careful balance between affirming her and sharing your perspective. When you don't validate at all, and instead challenge, deny, or ignore her feelings, your girl learns not to trust her internal gauge. When you do, she feels seen and witnessed.

What you don't want to do is try to fix things for her. Again, ask her open-ended questions. If she comes home upset by a friend, let her feel her emotions. Just hug her and let her know you are there for her for support. Then ask her what *she* thinks she should do. This builds her confidence that she can solve her problems herself and tells her she doesn't need an outside fix. And it shows you have trust in her. If your girl says she doesn't know, ask what she'd do if she *did* know. If still nothing, that's okay, too. Tell her it'll come. She'll know.

You can even take it a step further after validation and acknowledge who she's *being* in the moment—e.g., you're such a loyal friend, a responsible person, a caring big sister—and watch her heart open as she expands into that space. *Then* appeal to her sensibilities such as how to fix the problem, what to do differently next time, what the takeaways are, and how to bounce back.

Coaching Exercise—Thoughts as Emotional Fuel

Notice with your girl how different thoughts in her head produce different emotions in her body. For example, talk about how the thought "I have no friends" makes her feel differently than thinking "I have great friends." You can do this with a variety of topics. At the end, ask her whether or not she thinks she controls her emotions, or the other way around.

Coaching Exercise—Retrospect Analysis

Think of an example where you were mad or sad on the outside, but on the inside, you were feeling something more tender. If there is an instance your girl actually witnessed, break it down with her and show her your tender "first" feeling. Ask your girl if she has any examples where she had an inner, tender feeling, and ask her to similarly break it down.

Coaching Exercise—Raise the Vibe

I explain to my girls that all your thoughts and feelings are energy, and energy is vibration—your "vibe." Learn to raise those vibrations and watch your life change dramatically. Also, nurturing your own vibe is probably one of the best things you can do for the special girl in your life. She's a sponge, watching what you do and taking it *all* in!

Here are some quick boosters:

1. Find something beautiful and appreciate it.
2. Make a list of all that you are grateful for.
3. Meditate.
4. Do something for someone else.
5. Stop complaining and gossiping.
6. Move. Exercise. Get active.

7. Realize you have more control over your life than you thought.
8. Breathe.
9. Do something that scares you.
10. Have a meaningful conversation with a friend.

A Coaching Moment

One way to bolster your daughter's confidence is to increase her self-awareness and ability to trust her inner emotions. You can start by using more feeling words yourself. But then also help *her* to further articulate what's going on inside at any given moment. For instance, on the way to the pool one day, I surveyed my girls: "So, how's everyone feeling today?" They both just said "good." Instead of stopping there, I then asked them to be more specific. And between the two of them, they came back with the answers, *happy, active, full of energy, and powerful!*

It *can* be that simple. And by doing this, you're teaching your girl how to check in with and understand herself more and more. Pretty cool, right?!

Notes

Chapter 7

TAKE RISKS
AND STAND OUT

Y ou may have heard the quote, "Feel the fear and do it anyway." Healthy risk-taking is the true muscle of confidence building

What matters is the reward, not the result.

because it gets you outside your comfort zone to stretch yourself and your expectations. When you demonstrate courage, you build trust—trusting yourself that you can do "it" and trusting that you can handle the outcome if things don't go the way you thought or hoped they would. Whether or not you are successful is almost irrelevant because the simple act of trying something new or differently grows your confidence muscles. Standing out is also a healthy risk that can contribute to the strength of those muscles. Just like a muscle in your arm or leg, the more you exercise it, the stronger it gets!

As humans, we all take risks at one time or another. Some people are more drawn to unknown outcomes than others. Adolescents in particular are hardwired for this. But what's important is to be taking the *right* risks. Most people associate the term "risk" with the negative—like drinking, drugs, or sex. But there is positive or healthy risk-taking, which is actually good for you and good for your girl. In fact, positive risk-taking not only builds self-confidence, but it can also prevent negative risk-taking behavior because it satisfies the urge for thrill seeking. Things like playing team sports, volunteering, and making new friends are all examples of positive risk-taking behavior.

Our family has recently started rock-climbing together. What makes this activity risky is that it includes the possibility of failure. But it's in failing that we grow. Plus, kids need to learn to win *and* lose. In fact, it's probably more important to learn the latter because we will lose many more times in life than we will win. It's easy to be confident when you're winning. The real challenge is to be able to still believe in yourself when things aren't going your way. A useful reframe I tell my kids is that **you're either winning or you're learning.**

Remember that your role model status comes into play here. As girls get older, many negative risk-taking behaviors can be avoided by paying attention to your own patterns. Model taking healthy risks. This is especially important in today's world because girls feel enormous pressure to be perfect, which makes it harder and harder for them to be themselves and accept mistakes. Perfection is not the point—for her or you. Take positive risks, and she will follow your example.

"Perfection is not the point, for her or you."

A healthy risk is an action you desire to do that is out of your comfort zone and has an unknown outcome—a positive risk carries a chance of failure. It's not easy to take on that possible failure, and that's why we fear it. It makes us vulnerable. But you know what? Vulnerability and personal power are flip sides of a coin. Our mistakes make us stronger and help us make better decisions next time. Teach your girl to stretch herself rather than be bound by her comfort zone.

What's even more important is modeling a healthy response to failure and bouncing back. We grasp this concept intuitively when our kids learn to walk. They tumble, and a look of fear from us signals danger, causing her to cry. A calm reaction gets baby back on her feet. This way of dealing with failure is so meaningful that the next chapter is devoted to it!

The other way to build confidence muscles with your actions is to stand out. There's just no question about it; we draw self-confidence from the things we're good at or passionate about—gaining status for being good at something brings a great deal of confidence with it, too. Because of this, it is imperative to help your girl find her strong suit. If it seems like there isn't anything, keep looking. Follow whatever clues you see and let her lead the way.

It is *vitally* important you let her lead this charge. While our girls watch our every move and you are her primary role model, don't bear the whole burden of who she becomes. Part of role modeling is to remain open-minded. What I mean by this is that your girl's best version of herself may not be the same best version *you* have in mind for her. Our job is not to guide our girls into becoming a "mini-me." Instead, help open her eyes to what it is to be a woman living confidently on purpose.

You can do this by exposing your girl to a variety of strong, passionate women in a diversity of settings doing many different things. If she likes art, bring her to your artist friend's studio. If politics is appealing, take her on a trip to meet her congressional representative. Or if she loves helping people, introduce her to local soup kitchen organizers, therapists, or nurses. Let your girl determine the best version of herself, and you will be appreciated for genuinely great modeling, even if she doesn't realize it at the time.

Coaching Exercise—Healthy Risk Plan

Come up with a healthy risk plan for yourself, for your girl, or even for you to tackle together. The risks don't have to be big, and they should be age-appropriate. They should also be something you desire to do, not something that you're being forced to do. They should be outside your comfort zone, meaning there's a sense of exciting fear or it makes you catch your breath. And there should be an unknown outcome, a chance you could fail.

They can be pretty simple acts like calling in a pizza order for the first time. With little kids, what new and cool things do they want to try? With older girls, talk to them about classes, clubs, and sports and identify goals for each and ways to reach them. Talk about how to achieve their goal within their comfort zone and then within their risk zone. You can make this a fun part of your journey together. Maybe do a challenge per week. You can also look at your calendar of what's coming up and ask, "What is the risk?" Push the envelope a little each time.

Set a deadline. **If you succeed, celebrate. If you fail, still celebrate**. What's important is the attempt. Make sure to note the reward (the big picture), not the result (small picture). For example, what did she learn? How will she integrate this into her self-framework?

Also look for opportunities for explicit recognition or acknowledgment of her attempts. It can be a ribbon or an announcement, but it can also be a photo or the "you are special plate" at dinner—something to commemorate the event. Use it as a tangible, reinforcing reminder of what she did and the fear she overcame in the process.

If your girl is scared of potential failure, don't be afraid to give her a pep talk! Amy Baltzell, who coordinates the sports psychology program at Boston University, gives advice on how to do this. Already finding myself fumbling through these types of conversations with my own kids, I was instantly interested in her work—who doesn't want to help their kids do their best in an event? Baltzell's guidance is first to ask your girl how she's feeling and normalize it by telling her it's normal to be nervous, scared, etc.

Next, review what practice and preparation she's done already. By shifting focus to your child's efforts (studying, practicing) instead of the results (winning, succeeding), you'll help her develop a growth mindset and believe in her potential to improve and succeed (see Chapter 8 for more on a growth mindset). Then, inquire about specific things she's nervous about and what strategies she can use to help. Warming her brain up for the task ahead is priming her for success. Finally, tell her to keep things in perspective. At the end of the day, you love her no matter how things turn out.

Coaching Exercise—
It's More than Okay to Stand Out

Show your girl it's cool to stand out. It's a risk to put yourself out there, and this is especially exaggerated in adolescence. Social pressures often dictate that girls blend in and not be noticed. Girls can think that a spotlight shining on them is bragging and only makes others feel worse. They, then, don't want to be center stage. Indeed, it can also make them a target for negative attention. Margaret just found this out when she ran for (and won) student body president. It was the first time a fourth grader was allowed to compete, and she beat out nine fifth graders in the process. Unfortunately, a few of her opponents, as well as an unrelated group of fifth-grade boys, resorted to teasing her about it. This is such a shame and I tell Margaret not to get hooked by these real-life gremlins. (See more about how we're dealing with this in Chapter 10.) Instead, teach your girl that for every naysayer out there, there are ten more who are inspired by her brave actions. I can't tell you how many girls and moms came up to me after Margaret's winning speech to say how excited they were and how they wanted to join us in our confidence-building workshops.

Furthermore, shining her light does not mean going around saying "I'm the best" or "I'm the smartest, fastest," you fill in the blank. Some younger girls do talk like this, and it does make others feel bad because you're lifting yourself up by putting others down. Acceptable self-praise is saying something like, "I'm really proud of myself for..." or, "I'm happy with the way I did x or y."

Pay attention to a time when you can tell your girl is proud of herself. Play it up big time. Then tell your adult friends, too, so they can mention it to her when they see her. Compounding her feelings about something she's already feeling great about will leapfrog her confidence!

But also teach your girl to be sensitive if she knows a friend is struggling in an area where she succeeds. It could feel like she's rubbing it in if your girl is talking herself up in that friend's presence. Teach her the balance between the two, but be sure to emphasize self-praise, since the societal pressure is to deemphasize it. Work through these questions with her:

1. What do you think you're good at?
2. What do you love doing so much that you don't notice time passing?
3. How can you be proud of yourself for these things?
4. What does it mean to you to toot your own horn?
5. When do you think it's okay/not okay to do it?

Coaching Exercise—The Jealousy Sign-Post

Jealousy is harmful and can be challenging. But, if we change our perspective, jealousy can show us what we admire about someone or want for ourselves in the future. Explain to your girl that if someone does get jealous of her, or if your girl is envious of someone else, it's merely a sign that she wants the same thing for herself and her friend just helped her identify that. She should, in fact, be thanking her! As Glennon Doyle of Momastery says, "Envy is just unexpressed admiration. It's respect holding its breath. We're only envious of those already doing what we were meant to do." She says it's "a giant flashing arrow pointing us toward our destiny."

A Coaching Moment

I was reminded recently that confidence is not about the absence of fear. It's about feeling the fear and doing it anyway, like the quote that begins this chapter. When Elizabeth and I were rock climbing, she was very nervous and didn't want to go to the top. Then she did it anyway. And when she got down, I said, "Elizabeth you did it! You overcame your fear!" She replied, "I know! But I was still super scared!" And that's the lesson. Some people think that those with confidence never feel fear. But that's not true. They feel fear (or doubt, or self-pity) just like the next person. But they decide not to let it stop them.

Another Coaching Moment

I tried Amy Baltzell's steps in a small way one day when Elizabeth, who was six at the time, told me she was scared to go to soccer because she'd missed the previous week's practice. I immediately thought of Baltzell's advice and said, "That's totally normal to feel nervous." Next, I reminded her that all of the running and playing she'd been doing during her time off would serve her well. Then I asked her what moves she remembered from last soccer practice, and she started listing them off. I didn't ask her what she's specifically nervous about because I could already hear the confidence rising in her voice. She ended up having a super practice!

A Third Coaching Moment

When my girls were younger, they would see something in someone else that they too wanted to have or do—like the ability to ride bikes no-handed, move up a reading level in class, or even get a new haircut. Instead of feeling jealousy or casting negative energy upon that person, they quite surprisingly took it as the clear message that that thing, that achievement, or that quality was something they could and should have or do. They were able to honestly compliment that person and move on, as if to say, "Thank you very much for inspiring me to go for it, too!"

Several years ago, Elizabeth finally learned a trick on the monkey bars that Margaret had been able to do but she couldn't. Since she was so used to hearing my confidence sound bites, she said to me, "Look, Mom, I can finally do the monkey bars like Maggie. I was so jealous of her, but that's just because it was something I wanted to do, too!" It becomes so much harder for us to do this as we grow up, but, if we can, we must remind ourselves that jealousy is just a signpost of what's next for us in life.

Notes

Chapter 8

FAIL FORWARD

Most folks have heard the term "growth mindset," popularized by Stanford professor and researcher Carol Dweck. It is the belief that you can grow smarter and increase any of your abilities with effort and hard work. More than anything, it's a way to take control of your learning, and it's **the power of "yet."** Do you think you're good at something, like math, basketball, or meeting new people? If not, simply tag the word "yet" onto your thought, and suddenly you're standing in a new perspective. A growth mindset is another key to self-confidence for girls and women on purpose.

"If parents want to give their children a gift, the best thing they can do is to teach them to love challenges, be intrigued by mistakes, enjoy effort, and keep on learning."
– Carol Dweck

The magic of this perspective is that it puts **the focus on the process rather than the result.** Decades of research show that hard work and dedication are the keys to success in school and life, not intellect and talent. The reason why this idea is essential is that the old school of thought insisted you needed inherent skill or intelligence to be good at something, which means your ability is innate or fixed. In other words, there's only so far you can go in your pursuits. This belief leaves you less resilient and vulnerable to failure because you see failure as a personal reflection. You're also more likely to develop a fear of challenges, be unmotivated to learn, and unwilling to remedy your shortcomings because you think, "What's the point?"

In contrast, a person with a growth mindset has fun learning, enjoys trying new things, isn't afraid to make mistakes, uses failure as a building block, and is inspired by others' success. When something gets hard, a growth mindset person says, "This may take some time," "I'll use a different strategy," and "I will learn how to do this."

The beautiful thing about a growth mindset is that it's based on the science of neuroplasticity. Neuroplasticity is brain flexibility and refers to the brain's ability to change as a result of experience. Unlike what was previously thought, the brain is more soft-wired than hard-wired. Our brains remain plastic for our entire lives, and it's now thought that the brain of a teenager is as pliable as a newborn's. How about that!

More specifically, in our brains are cells called neurons. When we learn a new activity, like math, singing, or riding a bike, these neurons talk to each other by sending electrochemical impulses. After two neurons "talk" once, the probability is higher that they'll talk again. (Just like new friends!) This next time is always much easier and faster.

Eventually, the neurons will talk enough times that the brain considers it a priority pathway and it will take this route over any other. It wraps the pathway like a tortilla around a burrito with a fatty substance called myelin, making it even more permanent. Eventually and with consistent practice, this neural pathway becomes something automatic, like walking or talking. (See *The Power of Habit* (2014) by Charles Duhigg)

The brain's priority pathway-making process holds true for anything you're learning. It's also true for the beliefs you have about yourself, like we mentioned in Chapter 4 about gremlin thoughts. If you're thinking more and more negative thoughts, your brain will eventually build those bridges and they'll become automatic. But who wants that? Thankfully, it also works in reverse. The less you think a certain way, the less-used that pathway becomes, and the brain follows it decreasingly. You can train your brain. If you want to think more positive thoughts, then intentionally think positive thoughts more. If you want to think fewer negative thoughts, refuse to dwell on the ones that show up. Where you focus your attention grows.

"Where you focus your attention grows."

With this knowledge you can help your girl see her brain as a learning machine and that she is in control of developing it. This empowers her and teaches her not to limit her challenges, but to challenge her limits.

You can start to influence your girl's mindset today by teaching her to see everyday challenges as fun and exciting. Also, begin to emphasize that things that are "perfect" or "easy" are boring. This helps her be more open-minded. She will begin to see that there are many ways to be successful, that correct answers come in many forms, and that failing is not moving backward.

In fact, failing is the best way to be successful or to learn. In the fifth-grade corridor of my daughters' school hangs the quote, "Instead of saying 'Oops,' say 'Aha!'" Our kids' mindsets toward failure lie not in the big moments, but in the small ones. Take, for instance, when I broke a glass doing the dishes. Instead of saying "Oops" and getting annoyed with myself, I could have said "Aha!" and reacted with curiosity. I could have verbalized my thoughts: "So that's what happens when I'm rushing," or "...when I let the sink get too full of dirty dishes," etc. I particularly think of perfectionist moms with this type of reaction because they never give themselves a break. But when we model giving ourselves more slack and then trade in the "Oops" for an "Aha," our kids will be more likely to do the same.

One thing to pay attention to is the reward in failures. You may say, "What? There's no such thing!" But believe me, there is. Think about this: your girl may not have gotten the part she auditioned for in the play, but she had the courage to try out. Failure is a regular part of life that is as beneficial as anything else. It is worthy of celebration because it means she took the risk, tried something new, and learned from it. This mindset also helps your girl to see the reward of her efforts rather than the result, like in Chapter 7. In sports, you can show her the reward is in the effort and not the results by emphasizing that you just love to watch her play. This is a process-focused approach, and it's big-picture oriented. Granted, it requires some stepping back to see the forest for the trees, but that is a useful skill to have, too!

Use "process praise" to bring out the reward in her failures and encourage her resilience. Good phrases to use are: "I noticed how hard you worked on that," "You used great focus to achieve that task," or, "What might you try differently next time for another result?" Research shows that process praise has an even bigger impact on girls than boys because, from a young age, girls are more often emptily praised for their innate abilities and talents, like you're pretty, smart, etc. (See *Mindset* (2007) by Carol Dweck.) The impact of this on girls becomes obvious in adolescence, where girls don't show the skills or grit to persevere compared to their male counterparts. The difference is that boys have received specific feedback on their performance from a much younger age. (See *Grit* (2016) by Angela Duckworthy.) So celebrate failures! Use praise to highlight the effort and attempt, and see how much your girl grows.

Coaching Exercise—
What a Growth Mindset "Feels Like"

An exercise to do with your girl to see what it "feels" like to be in a growth mindset is to co-create a drawing, which I learned from a Khan Academy (www.khanacademy.org) demonstration. In this exercise, you take turns making a mark on a piece of paper without raising your pen and without speaking. Keep taking turns until you feel your drawing is complete. You may even give it a title! Once you're done, talk about the thoughts that went through your head. Did your drawing turn out the way you expected or wanted it? Was it frustrating at first? At some point, did you "let go" and go with the flow? Did you stay open-minded and flexible? Did you keep going and not quit? Did you have fun? This is what it feels like to have a growth mindset whenever you're learning a new activity or doing something hard!

Next, make an extensive list of everything you don't think you're good at. Write them out in sentence form such as "I'm not good at drawing." After you're done, go back and write the word "yet" after each statement, shifting the thought into a growth mindset. How does that shift the way you feel?

Coaching Exercise—Fail Forward

We need to learn how to think of failure differently because the common perception is *so* negative. A rule we have in our confidence workshops is to high-five each other and say something like, "You rock!" or "You're so cool!" whenever we make a mistake. The reason we do this is to get girls to think about failure in a new way. When we make a mistake, it's an opportunity to learn something in an accelerated, fresh way. We typically pull our posture down in frustration or embarrassment, but high-fives open up our bodies, expanding them to help us feel more confident!

You can also try thinking of mistakes as the two words: "my" and "stake." What is a "stake"? One definition is something you can gain or lose, like in a game or contest. Have you ever heard the phrase "What's at stake?" "What are the stakes?" or "Raise the stakes"? The "stake" you stand to gain or lose in any failure is a *lesson*. You can either gain that lesson or lose it. Again, it's a choice. Growth-mindset people learn from their mistakes and gain a lesson. Next time you make a mistake, ask yourself, "What is my stake?"

Coaching Exercise—Model and Celebrate Failures

You can model failing forward to help your girl embrace it, too. If you want to teach her to value it for real, start by sharing with her where you have failed. Tell her how you overcame whatever it was and what you learned from that experience. Or maybe you didn't overcome it and gave up. Tell her about that, too. You were once a child and should know that kids (below a certain age!) pretty much think their parents are perfect. So, knowing you did not succeed the first time at everything is going to mean more to her than any platitude. I'm not just talking about past failures. Share the current ones, too, and what you're doing about them.

Make it a habit to celebrate the day's failures at dinnertime. Take turns telling everyone about a problem you solved that day, what you did to figure it out, and how you overcame any blips. Or maybe you're still knee deep in it and haven't found the answer, but are persisting in your quest! Soon enough, she'll start to get that failing is part of the process. It moves you forward, not backward, and makes you better and stronger in the long run.

A Coaching Moment

I was playing checkers with my very competitive Maggie, and, despite her special rules (which constantly changed throughout the game), she was losing—and not happy about it! So, being me, I thought, *coaching moment?* I said, "Soooo, Maggie, what are some reasons other than winning that you might play a game?" After serious eye rolling, squirming, and prodding, she began a list: to have fun, to spend time with Mom, to learn something new, to teach someone something, to be happy for the other person if they win. A pretty good list, I thought. Now I'm not sure she bought the lesson that there are reasons to play equally important to winning, but what I can tell you is that this simple exercise completely changed the tone of our game and we went on to have the absolute best time! I've noticed that brainstorming is an easy way to remember that we always have choices—in what we do, say, and think, and in our attitude. And it can help to shift your focus away from the result and into a growth mindset. Try brainstorming with *your* girl and see what happens!

Another Coaching Moment

I regularly ask my girls, "What's one brave thing you did today?" in the hope that they learn to recognize even the smallest feats. Several years ago, I asked my usual question and my oldest replied, "Nothing really." I instantly started searching for possibilities to hand her. I decided to capitalize on the only extraordinary thing we had done that day: going to the theater. I said, "Well, you went to see a new movie other than Frozen." (We'd seen it three times by that point . . .) "And, you carried the popcorn all the way for the first time in the dark and didn't spill!" As you can tell, I was grasping at straws.

As usual, Margaret kept me on my toes. "Mom, doing *new* things isn't the same as doing *brave* things." Hmm, I thought. Is that true? And I started to defend myself. But you know, I think she's right. New and brave may be the same sometimes, but not always. A courageous act is when you're at least a little bit scared. By this definition, seeing a new movie and carrying popcorn definitely don't qualify. But the more significant lesson I learned is how **kids can see right through our empty praise!** Especially when it's for normal or expected behavior. Kids only want credit where credit is due. In fact, false praise could even have the unintended consequence of lowering their expectations of themselves, and we certainly don't want that. So here's to kids teaching us lessons, to the brave and not-so-brave things, to knowing the difference, and to accepting that neither needs to happen every day.

To the contrary, pay attention to when your girl is feeling proud of something she's done that *was* brave, and lay it on thick! Your girl's confidence will skyrocket.

Notes

Chapter 9

LEARN TO GROUND

Just like your girl needs help finding her core values framework (Chapter 3), she also needs your help to feel grounded. Did you know that the brain's frontal lobe, responsible for all of our higher-order thinking (like decision-making), is not fully developed until the age of twenty-five? It should come as no surprise that your girl needs to feel connected to *you* in particular to feel confident. You are her primary grounding pole.

> "Nothing can bring you peace but yourself."
>
> - Ralph Waldo Emerson

One of the ways to help your girl feel grounded or centered is to really "get" her. Again, just like finding her core values framework, take the time to hug and snuggle, and intently listen to your girl. These actions strengthen your bond because they happen in the deep limbic system, where attachment circuitry lives and where emotion is regulated. When your relationship is healthy, your girl does better, learns more, and makes friends more easily. When this attachment is off, she's going to flounder.

Another reason our girls' brains need us is for something called "mirroring" or "affect matching." When an especially young child is upset, and an adult mirrors their emotion (as in, we show a replica on our face of what they're feeling), it stimulates their mirror neuron cells, which release opiates, endorphins, and oxytocin. These hormones engage their frontal lobe so they can *respond* to their environment instead of merely reacting. Oxytocin is otherwise known as the love and trust hormone, and it's

> "Your girl needs to feel connected to YOU to feel confident."

what makes us feel connected. This is vital to our kids' brains in times of distress. When we simply come in and try to fix their problems, change the subject, or just say, "What's wrong?" (I'm guilty of this!), we're furthering the fight-or-flight state they're already experiencing.

By mirroring, it's not what you say but how you say it that matters. Whether you paraphrase your girl, say the same thing back to her, clarify or summarize what she said, or just wonder out loud, mirroring is not about agreeing, but about stepping into your girl's shoes and letting her know on your face that you understand. This starts the oxytocin chain reaction, according to Jennifer Kolari, family therapist and author of *Connected Parenting: How to Raise a Great Kid* (2010). This is all to say that our kids regulate off of our frontal lobe, and the emotional soil we till can have a dramatic impact on their brain. This is the ultimate task for moms as role models. It looks a little something like this: When your girl is stressing out, calmly make three or four statements to show you get it. For example, "You're feeling frustrated," "This is hard," or "It doesn't seem fair." In other words, echo her experience to her. She will begin to adjust to an oxytocin moment because she's no longer pumping adrenaline. Then, step back and guide the incredible coaching moment you now have with your girl!

As much as your girl depends on you to feel grounded, you also want to give her tools to ground herself when you're not around. As a result, she'll feel more in control of her life and more confident. Cutting through the stress we have every day can bring an ease that's central to self-confidence.

As I mentioned in Chapter 4, some describe confidence as a natural state for everyone, not something to build but something to return to. We see it with toddlers learning to walk, talk, or eat for the first time. They confidently go for what they want and may fail, but use mistakes and failures as information to course correct and continue. We start to alter this process in childhood and throughout our lives, forming habitual patterns where we get pulled aside, or *hooked*, by all kinds of insecure thoughts like, "I can't," or "I don't know how." Since our emotions reflect our thoughts, we end up repeatedly overriding our natural confidence.

If you explain this to your girl, you'll see how quickly she gets it. Explain that there's nothing wrong with her and that her core is strong. She is already naturally creative, resourceful, and whole! And her self-doubt is simply a thought passing through like clouds. Once she can identify the insecure thoughts, that makes them visible to her, giving her a chance to not engage with them when they occur. This is an effective way she can learn to ground.

The other way we teach the girls in our workshops to ground themselves is through meditation. Meditation is an excellent way to manage stress and clear your mind. This practice will allow your girl to retreat and clear her mind when life gets stressful.

Coaching Exercise—Pictured Feelings

It may help you better understand your girl if you know how she perceives her emotions. Ask her, "What does it feel like inside when you're really upset?" Then have her draw a picture of this feeling. The next time you're "grounding" her, use the words she chose, so she knows you get her problem.

Coaching Exercise—Leaves on a Stream

Girls can learn how to meditate at a very young age. We have found that breathing techniques are particularly useful. We've used the buddha breath to help our kids overcome stress by getting out of their mind and into their body. One of my favorite meditative exercises is a cognitive defusion visualization adapted from Russ Harris' *Leaves on a Stream* in *The Confidence Gap*. Cognitive defusion is letting go of your thoughts—especially those that are causing you harm. You can use it to clear your mind anytime, anywhere: when you're sad or nervous, you need to focus more, or you're just having trouble falling asleep. Feel free to adapt this for your girl however you like, and adjust it for yourself, too. You may find it quite useful! The exercise goes like this:

1. Sit in a comfortable position and either close your eyes or rest them gently on a fixed spot in the room.

2. Picture your favorite tree. It can be a real tree in your yard or one you've seen in a book or a movie. You can also make your tree up. *Pause for ten seconds.*

3. What does your tree look like? Does it have leaves, flowers, fruits? What season is it?

4. Now visualize a gently flowing stream next to your tree. Floating along the surface of the water are leaves, flowers, or fruits that have fallen from your tree. *Pause for five seconds.*

5. For the next few minutes, take each thought that enters your mind and place it on a leaf (or flower, or fruit, etc.) that falls from your tree . . . Let it float by. Do this with each thought—positive,

negative, or neutral. Even if you have happy thoughts, place them on a leaf and let them fall and float past you.

6. If your thoughts momentarily stop, continue to watch the stream. Sooner or later, your thoughts will start up again. *Pause for ten seconds.*

7. Allow the stream to flow at its natural pace. Don't try to speed it up and rush your thoughts along. You're not trying to rush the leaves along or "get rid" of your thoughts. You are allowing them to come and go at their own pace.

8. If your mind says, "This is dumb," "I'm bored," or, "I'm not doing this right," place *those thoughts* on leaves, too, and let them pass. *Pause for ten seconds.*

9. If a leaf gets stuck, allow it to hang around until it's ready to float by. If the thought comes up again, watch it float by another time. *Pause for ten seconds.*

10. If a difficult feeling arises, simply acknowledge it. Say to yourself, "I notice myself feeling bored/impatient/frustrated." Place those thoughts on leaves and allow them to fall and float along.

11. From time to time, your thoughts may hook you and distract you from being fully present in this exercise. This is *normal.* Gently bring your

attention back to the visualization exercise as soon as you realize that you have become sidetracked.

12. Now imagine your stream is slowing down into a smaller tributary, then a brook, and then it becomes just a trickle of water. Finally, it opens up into a beautiful, wide, open, placid lake. You may now open your eyes.

In our coaching workshops, I have the girls draw what their personal tree looks like at the end of the visualization and then take it home to keep right next to their bed at night. I tell them their trees can look any way they want. They can be real or imagined. They can have leaves, or flowers, or money falling from them. I've even had girls imagine trees made of chocolate and soccer balls! The point is just for them to learn to actively place their thoughts on each leaf/flower/chocolate bar/soccer ball as it falls into the stream and floats away.

Ask these questions afterward: "What did this meditation mean to you?" and "How are you and your thoughts separate from each other?"

We tell the girls to put their tree by their beds because often we become flooded with thoughts at night. Leaves on a Stream is a great way to calm those thoughts and prepare for rest. For the girl who has a hard time turning off her mind at bedtime, try these tricks too:

1. Walk her through a visualization of a favorite place, ending with her lying down on a grassy hill, a beach, or any other place of her choosing, and then describe the feeling of the warmth of the sun on each part of her body.
2. Teach her to lie completely still in her bed and try to feel the energy in her fingertips, then in her hands. Keep going until she's gone through her entire body.
3. Tell her that if she has to, get up and draw a simple picture or symbol of each thing on her mind so that it is no longer in her head.
4. Make her a calming jar to look at (glitter, glue, food coloring, and water) until she's ready to fall asleep.

A Coaching Moment

A friend told me she's been "grounding" her kids a lot lately. Her eight-year-old daughter gets frustrated to the point where she says she "feels like she needs to bite something." This is when she usually lashes out by either yelling, being mean to her siblings, or pushing someone. She explains to her daughter that she has every right to all of her emotions but what's not okay is hurting herself or others as a result. A few weeks ago, one of these moments came up while she was playing in her bedroom. After my friend repeated her usual lesson on emotions and was exiting the room, her daughter looked at her with desperation in her eyes and blurted, "Well, what do I do with all my anger then?!" She could tell she wasn't giving her enough tools or options. So she went back in and sat down next to her on her bed. They talked about how to ground ourselves. They talked about emotions just being energy in motion. They talked about how to move your body to move the energy through us. And they talked about taking deep breaths and practiced right then and there. With each breath out, she asked her daughter to imagine letting go of a little bit of anger each time.

Notes

Chapter 10

CHOOSE
YOUR COMMUNITY

W hen I cover self-confidence and community in my workshops, I'm usually talking about friendships and the people with whom we get to choose to spend time. Inevitably, when I ask girls, "Who here thinks you should be friends with everyone?" they *all* raise their hands. Some look around to see who else is going to say yes, too, but, generally speaking, this is what girls think. They equate not being friends with someone as being "mean." That's when I explain that just because you don't choose to be friends with someone, it doesn't mean you shouldn't still treat them with respect and kindness. Treat everyone with kindness, but choose your close friends with discernment. They have a massive effect on your life.

"Your best friends bring out your best."

- Henry Ford

Carefully choosing friends is important because we become like those with whom we surround ourselves. Think of a child who never chases her dreams because of her risk-averse family, or even a young adult who limits her goals because all her friends are settling (in their career, love life, etc.). Misery loves company. But so does confidence. If you want to be more confident in your life, it is essential that you limit your time with people who lack self-confidence and find people who build you up. If the first step is not realistic—for example, you have a negative family member always shooting down your ideas—at least have the smarts not to tell them your delicate hopes and

> "Find your tribe."

dreams. Secondly, find your tribe. True confidence cannot exist in a vacuum; for it to grow and flourish, you need a community to support you in all of your possibility. Together, you and your tribe can strive to be girls and women on purpose, and help each other all along the way! It's a lot easier with the right friends.

Always be on the lookout for friends to make that tribe, ones that build your girl up and don't bring her down. These girls are the ones who are not afraid to stand out and be good at something. Girls who know who they are and have healthy self-esteem. Girls who see the potential in both themselves and your daughter and are not afraid to fail. It is your job to steer her toward the best community for her. At the same time, you want to have confidence in your girl's ability to choose the right friends for her and coach her how to do this.

Talk to your girl about this exactly: what to look for in a friend, how to find it, and that it's okay not to be friends with everyone. In our confidence workshops, we teach girls about the Law of Attraction and that by being a good friend, you will likely attract good friends. Important traits to look for in others include someone who is fun to be with, is trustworthy, and is kind and respectful. In addition, a good friend is inclusive, supportive, fights fair (using "I" statements instead of accusatory "you" statements), and knows how to say sorry. Girls not worth your attention are those that get jealous instead of being happy for you, don't share, threaten to take away their friendship, tease (often followed by "just kidding"), gossip, and give the silent treatment. A client's nine-year-old daughter recently had an experience where she found out a new girl at school who she had made a special effort to befriend and welcome into the community was talking about her behind her back. True friends don't do this and, while she continues to treat this girl with kindness and respect, she decided she probably isn't the type of friend she's looking for right now. If you can help your girl learn how to *actively* choose the people in her life, people who make her feel relaxed and comfortable with herself, it will help her not only with finding true friends now but later with romantic partners, too.

Also, be sure to talk to your girl about having friends in many places or parts of her life. Girls can be catty and cliquey, and one day your daughter may find herself un-friended by an entire group for no good reason. And it will be hard on her. Having other groups to soften the blow will be critical. Plus, having a variety of friends teaches your girl that there are many aspects of her personality that no one group or person can fulfill at all times. Diversity is a good thing; it expands her interests and intelligence.

We tell girls in our workshops that having different kinds of friends is like having different types of shoes. You wouldn't wear soccer cleats to a school dance, just like you wouldn't invite your friend who prefers to stay in and watch movies to go with you to a rowdy concert. Fortify your girl's confidence by encouraging her to develop and nurture friendships with many different groups and types of people. Even exposing her to a variety of interests can do the trick. Sign her up for a sports team, an acting class, and a book club. She's bound to find a cross-section of girls in all three!

Another important way to vary your girl's support tribe is to find mentors and cheerleaders for her. While we as parents have the best intentions, the reality is that our girls may not always be able to "hear" messages from us. For this reason, it's extremely important to find other adults in your family's orbit who you see regularly, who she responds to, and who have your girl's back. Talk to these people and share with them the messages you are trying to reinforce with your girl. Ask them to pepper their interactions with her with the same messages. This will have a powerful, reinforcing impact on your girl because she'll be getting support from multiple angles. This will make her strong, even when she faces adversity.

Though she may feel solid in her tribe, trouble always comes, and it's still hard. The most common forms trouble takes are peer pressure and bullying. Peer pressure is not always a bad thing, but girls need to know what it is and how to handle it. We tell girls in our workshops that sometimes people do things they don't want to do because they want to fit in, belong, or be accepted. And this is totally normal! But next time your friend is trying to get you to do something you're not ready to do, you aren't comfortable doing, or you just don't feel is right, one way to deal with it is to put on your "I choose to" glasses from Chapter 5 and make a choice that's right for *you*. This lesson would have come in handy for one of the girls who teased Margaret after the election, because this girl went along with it even though it wasn't her idea. She had succumbed to peer pressure because she wanted to be liked by one of the other girls. Later, realizing this wasn't who she is or wanted to be, she courageously came over to our house and apologized, showing great care and integrity instead. Remember: confidence comes from the courage to be who *you* are, not who someone else is—even your friends.

Peer pressure is easier to deal with than bullying. With bullying, your girl has to be brave to stop it in its tracks. Natalia's bullying story from Chapter 4 eroded not only *her* self-esteem but that of the entire team. A bully in a community is like a virus that will infect everyone. **Standing up to that bully is the only way to stop her.** Natalia finally had a moment of clarity when she witnessed that girl bullying someone else. Once she told the girl her behavior was not okay, the girl stopped! Earlier I mentioned the backlash Margaret faced as a result of winning her school election. In particular, a small group of fifth-grade boys started mocking her. While I would actually consider this harassment[viii] because they are older and boys, we talked about it in the same way we might talk about bullying. Margaret told me she didn't quite know how to handle it, so we brainstormed. Some ideas we came up with were 1. Ignore it; 2. Deflect it with humor; 3. Tell them to stop; 4. Go the principal. She did not like the last point because she said she feels like she's old enough and should be able to take care of things on her own. This is mistaken thinking that a lot of girls believe. No one should ever feel like they need to handle anything all by themselves and they should always ask for help if they need it.

We decided to give it a week because the frequency of incidents was starting to die down. But then, just a few days later, Margaret came home so excited with news she couldn't wait to tell me. She said, "Guess what? At recess I unexpectedly found myself in the sports equipment shed with those fifth-grade boys." "Uh oh," I replied. "Then the ring leader said, 'Hey, are you our President?' and I said, 'Yes,' and then he started clapping and sarcastically cheering, 'Go President! Go President!'" "What did you do?" I asked her. Margaret said, "I told him to please stop!" "Oh my gosh, Margaret! Congratulations! And then what did they do?" She paused and continued, "The lead boy said, 'Okay' in an embarrassed voice, put his head down and then walked out with the other boys behind him!" The bottom line is the only way to truly stop bullying is to address it head on with either a firm "STOP" or by getting adults involved.

Be sure to teach your girl that it's not enough to just notice bullying; she has to stand up and say something when she sees it.

Coaching Exercise—Sharing Circle

We end all of our workshops with a sharing circle so that the girls experience what it feels like to support and be supported by community. We each take turns telling each other something we admire and then in response the receiver replies, "Thank you." The exercise is important not only because it teaches girls how to directly build each other up, but the "Thank you" also shows them how to respectfully accept a verbal gift, thereby building up the giver. Finally, by saying "Thank you" to a compliment, girls learn to take more ownership of their awesomeness. It's an all-around win-win. You can practice doing this directly with just your girl, at the dinner table with the family, or you can teach her to do it with her friends!

A Coaching Moment

If your girls are anything like mine, they bicker. And sometimes they bicker with their really close friends who, for all intents and purposes, are like sisters. When Margaret was eight years old, she was playing with one of her good friends creating an imaginary Olympic event, complete with judges, contestants, and prizes. I noticed she would always follow her friend's ideas with "no, let's do the scoring by (insert her idea)" or "no, the prize is (insert her idea again)," etc. Her friend was taking it quite well, sometimes objecting to the repeated rejections, but there was clearly tension in the air. So, I simply suggested to her, "Maggie, instead of saying 'No' and then stating your idea, try saying 'Yes, and...' followed by your idea!" And I swear the change was instantaneous—the creativity began to flow between them, they started building each other up and expanding their ideas, and I could see the validation in her friend's face. Then the fun really began.

Another Coaching Moment

Girls can be mean. I didn't think it could happen this early, but Elizabeth was bullied back when she was in preschool. Perhaps it happened unintentionally, or was partly excusable as normal behavior for that age as kids learn to assert their dominance. All I knew was that my little Elizabeth never wanted to go to school and would come home deflated every day. She was obsessed with whatever this particular child did or said to her.

One afternoon, she came home sulking. "Everybody was mean to me today," she complained. "No one wanted to play with me. It was the worst day ever." Once we sat down and talked about it, I realized it wasn't "everybody" but just this one girl. "Well, what is she saying or doing to you, Elizabeth?" I asked. "She's stealing Amelia away from me and then won't let me play with them." Hmmm, the usual guilty suspects with women: exclusion and the silent treatment. Some would argue this isn't bullying. But social aggression *is* on the bullying spectrum.

So, we talked about what her responses have been and what the teachers have told her to do (e.g., call the girl out on it, remind the girl of playground rules, go find someone else to play with, tell the teacher). But what really seemed to resonate was when I asked her, "So, Elizabeth, what do you look for in a friend?" She replied very quickly: Holly.

"Well, what is Holly like?" I prompted. "Fun, kindful (an Elizabeth original), adventurous, likes to do what I want to do first." "Well, great then," I said. "Now don't you want to play with someone who makes you feel good instead of bad?" Of course, she said, "Yes."

Then I told her a little story about when I was younger. "When I was in junior high school, all of the girls who I thought were my friends decided that I wasn't cool enough anymore and wouldn't hang around with me. It was hard and it made me feel sad. But you know what? That's when I found my new friends. And those same girls are still my friends to this day." When I finished my story, Elizabeth just wrapped her arms around me and gave me the biggest bear hug ever!

Next time you think your girl is struggling with friendships, try having a similar conversation. Sharing your stories will help her confidently live out hers.

Notes

FINAL THOUGHTS

Self-confidence is a tricky subject. We don't hesitate to talk about it for our girls and it's a totally trendy topic for today's kids. But have you noticed that at some point it

> If you ever feel like giving up, just remember there's a little girl watching who wants to be just like you.

becomes off-limits to talk about self-confidence as an adult? As grown-ups, lack of self-confidence becomes a dirty little secret we don't dare share. I want this to change. I want to start talking about self-confidence not just for girls but for women, too.

I had all the outward signs of self-confidence throughout my life—plenty of friends, did well at school, was a scholarship athlete, went to an Ivy League college, and landed a highly sought-after job with the EPA. However, even with all these "successes"—the kind any parent would want for their child—I never had confidence in myself. So many points along the way may have turned the course of my life, had I the confidence muscles to do what I want and be who I am.

I often think back to that humiliating moment in college with my professor. How might I have handled things differently? Perhaps I would have respectively stood up to her. Or had the perspective to request an after-hours meeting to voice my opinions. Maybe I would have had some opinions in the first place. Or even had the ability to sort out what I was feeling instead of just pushing it down and out of mind, my only true coping mechanism at the time. What would you hope your girl would do?

It wasn't until adulthood that I finally figured out how to be and do what I was meant for in the world, and I feel like I learned these things just in the nick of time. Every day I try to model this definition of self-confidence for my own girls, and you can, too.

There is no finish line. Building self-confidence is an ongoing, fine-tuning process. Even throughout writing this book I've had to consciously stay true to my core values of self-expression, connection, and making a difference. I've battled *many* gremlin thoughts. I've practiced meditation to stay focused. And I've only shared my dream with those who support me. I've always wanted to write a book, but showing it to the world scares me to death. It has required me to go *way* outside my comfort zone, and, truthfully, I never thought I'd go through with it. **What finally sealed the deal was my desire to continue role-modeling self-confidence and living on purpose for my daughters.**

Our girls need us, both as moms and as women. This is especially true in an overly competitive era, where they are scrutinized and held to impossible standards. Moreover, mistakes seem unforgivable in our society, causing depression and anxiety rates to go through the roof. We need a new definition of success that has nothing to do with being perfect, popular, or pretty; or getting the best grades; or going to the top college. The point is for our girls to be lit up, always learning, and fulfilled. This only comes from finding a personal definition of self-confidence: An ability to be who *you* are and to do what *you* want, irrespective of popular standards. **Girls on purpose need women on purpose.**

While moms set the primary example for girls, the call is even greater for women everywhere to role-model self-confidence. So coach yourself. Coach your girl. Coach your co-workers, your neighbors, your friends. Coach your friends' girls. Coach your friends' girls' friends. You get the idea! Spread the word that *anyone* can be and do all that they're meant for in the world. Anyone can live the life of a girl or woman on purpose. It's not hard, and it's **never** too late.

Our girls depend on it.

One Final Coaching Moment

One weekend many years ago, my kids and I walked down the road to feed some apples to Fancy, the neighborhood horse. We dropped two whole apples into his pen, but he only ate one, which happened to be the one I had. Elizabeth, who was five at the time, was so distraught that he wasn't eating hers, she started whining, "Fancy doesn't like me!" I said to her, "Elizabeth, you have no idea what Fancy's thinking. You can make this mean anything you want. It can mean he didn't see your apple. It can mean he was no longer hungry. It can mean he was saving it for later. Or it can mean he doesn't like you. Which are you going to choose?" These are the uncomplicated moments where our girls learn they are in control of how they see the world and see themselves.

After some time, we started walking away from our visit with Fancy and Elizabeth began to cry, "I just wanted him to eat my apple." I said, "Okay, now that's something to be upset about. I understand. I'm sorry, honey. But don't make yourself also feel bad by saying Fancy doesn't like you. Be nice to yourself. Ok? Be your own best friend." "Okay, Mama."

BE ON PURPOSE

I want to personally thank you for reading this book and making self-confidence a priority for you and your girl. I'd love to hear how these pages have impacted you. Please let me know at danielle@girl-onpurpose.com! Even better, I challenge you to form a Girl on Purpose Duo or Trio with your own girl(s) and work through every chapter of this book to build your self-confidence muscles together. *Even better* than that, I dare you to gather a Girl on Purpose Society with fellow Duos and Trios in your community, kind of like a book club, and realize the true power of tribes as you support each other in your shared journey! For more information on how to do this and to connect with me further, please visit www.girl-onpurpose.com.

NOTES

[i] "Gender stereotypes about intellectual ability emerge early and influence children's interests" *Science*. 27 Jan 2017: Vol. 355, Issue 6323, pp. 389-391.

[ii] While girls have a hard time filling out their pie plates, Michelle Cove finds boys have a far easier time, announcing "I'm athletic!" "I'm smart!" "I'm funny!"

[iii] A fun activity to do with your girl after you've uncovered your values is to find a nice, smooth stone to represent her solid core. On one side, use markers to draw a picture of something she loves or loves doing; on the other side, write all the words that describe her reasons why. Have her squeeze her stone to demonstrate that her core never changes, even under pressure, like when her friends might be mad at her or she's in trouble with her parents. Encourage your girl to think of the rock as a physical reminder of who she is at her core and put it somewhere special.

[iv] Creswell, Way, Eisenberger, Lieberman. "Neural Correlates of Dispositional Mindfulness During Affect Labeling." *Psychosomatic Medicine*, 2007, Vol. 69, pp. 560-565.

[v] I tell my students that the difference between two girls isn't whether or not they're having gremlin thoughts—it's whether or not they're getting hooked by them. You can have two girls trying out for the same school play and both are thinking "I'm going to forget my lines" or "She's so much better than me!" Only one gets hooked by her gremlin thoughts. Who do you think gets the part?

[vi] Kross et al. "Talk as a Regulatory Mechanism: How You Do It Matters." *Journal of Personality and Social Psychology*, American Psychological Association 2014, Vol. 106, No. 2, pp. 304-324.

[vii] While this is generally a true statement, it is an oversimplification of a more complex process.

[viii] Bullying usually results from jealousy and insecurity, whereas harassment is based on discrimination for perceived differences in gender, race, or religion. The latter is punishable under law.

Made in the USA
Monee, IL
08 January 2020